Table of Contents

On The Cover: This rainbow is over the Kenai River. A rainbow is an optical phenomenon that occurs when sunlight and conditions in the atmosphere are just right. Light enters a water droplet, slowing down and bending as it goes from air to denser water. The light reflects off the inside of the droplet, separating into its component wavelengths--or colors. When light exits the droplet, it makes a rainbow. https://scijinks.gov/

Genesis 9:12-17 And God said, This is the token of the covenant which I make between me and you and every living creature that is with you, for perpetual generations: 13 I do set my bow in the cloud, and it shall be for a token of a covenant between me and the earth. 14 And it shall come to pass, when I bring a cloud over the earth, that the bow shall be seen in the cloud: 15 And I will remember my covenant, which is between me and you and every living creature of all flesh; and the waters shall no more become a flood to destroy all flesh. 16 And the bow shall be in the cloud; and I will look upon it, that I may remember the everlasting covenant between God and every living creature of all flesh that is upon the earth. 17 And God said unto Noah, This is the token of the covenant, which I have established between me and all flesh that is upon the earth.

Cover design by *Elder Rashaun L. West*

A NOTE FROM THE SUPERINTENDENT

Grace and peace to you from our Lord Jesus Christ! As for God, his way is perfect: the word of the LORD is tried: he is a buckler to all those that trust in him, *Psalm 18:30.* The Lord is our shield, as iniquity continues to abound around us His Word is truth; tried and proven. As the world attempts to impose its viewpoint and values in our lives; we must abide in the Word of God. Jesus told those that believed on him if ye continue in my word, then are ye my disciples indeed. I pray this book communicates the truth and comfort of God's Word to you. Everyone is welcome and encouraged to attend Sabbath School. It is a great place to have fellowship and to learn the Word together. Thank you to all members of the compiling committee for your hard work and outstanding contributions to this book. Each author is noted at the end of each lesson, except the lessons I authored. Thank you to Apostle G.R. Dailey Jr. and the Apostle Board for their work in compiling this book. If you have any questions, suggestions, or feedback regarding the lessons, please contact me at: brohurst@houseofgod.org

In Christ's Love,

Bro. Joshua Hurst, National Sabbath School Superintendent

House of God Sabbath School Lessons

HOLY CHURCH OF THE LIVING GOD
THE PILLAR AND THE GROUND OF THE TRUTH
THE HOUSE OF PRAYER FOR ALL PEOPLE
(Hebrew Pentecostal)

The Late Bishop R. A. R. Johnson, D.D., M.B., Founder
The Late Bishop A. A. Smith, D.D., Ph.D., first Chief Apostle
The Late Bishop S. P. Rawlings, B.S., Th.D., 2nd Chief Apostle
The Late Bishop F. C. Scott, D.D., Chief Apostle
Apostle James E. Embry, Jr. Chief Apostle Emeritus
Apostle Thomas E. Clark, Chief Apostle

Sabbath School Superintendent: Brother Joshua Hurst
Assistant Superintendent: Evangelist Patricia Powell.

Compiling Committee: Brother Joshua Hurst, Evangelist Irene Crawford, Minister James Taylor, Elder James Fant, Evangelist Patricia Powell, Minister Robert O. Johnson

September 2022-September 2023

SABBATH SCHOOL ORDER OF SERVICE

Song by Congregation

Prayer whom he or she may designate

Responsive reading

Superintendent: Let my cry come near before Thee, O LORD give me understanding according to Thy word.

School: Let my supplication come before thee: deliver me according to Thy word.

Superintendent: My Lips shall utter praise when thou hast taught me thy statues.

School: My tongue shall speak of thy word for all thy commandments are righteousness.

Superintendent: Let thine hand help me; for I have chosen thy precepts.

School: I have longed for thy salvation; O LORD and thy law is my delight.

Superintendent: Let my soul live, and it shall praise thee; and let thy judgments help me.

School: I have kept thy precepts and thy testimonies: for all my ways are before thee.

Superintendent: Teach me, O LORD, the way of thy statutes; and I shall keep it unto the end.

School: Give me understanding, and I shall keep thy law: yea, I shall observe it with my whole heart.

Superintendent: Make me to go in the path of thy commandments; for therein do I delight.

School: Incline my heart unto thy testimonies, and not to covetousness.

Superintendent: Turn away my eyes from beholding vanity; and quicken thou me in thy way.

School: Stablish thy word unto thy servant, who is devoted to thy fear.

Superintendent: Turn away my reproach from which I fear: for thy judgments are good.

School: Behold, I have longed after thy precepts: quicken me in thy righteousness.

Superintendent: Wherewithal shall a young man cleanse his way? By taking heed thereto according to thy word.

School: My son, forget not my law, but let thine heart keep my commandments:

Superintendent: For length of days, and long life, and peace, shall they add to thee.

School: Let not mercy and truth forsake thee: bind them about thy neck; write them upon the table of thine heart.

Superintendent: So shalt thou find favor and good understanding in the sight of God and man.

School: Trust in the LORD with all thy heart; and lean not unto thine own understanding.

All: In all thy ways acknowledge him, and he shall direct thy paths.

Review of the principles
Classes arranged for study period
Classes report offering
Secretary's report
Lesson review
Receiving of members
Benediction

SABBATH SCHOOL SONG

Words by Elect Lady Mary Campbell, 1109 Prince Street, Beaufort, S.C.
To Be Sung in the Tune Of "We've Come This Far by Faith"
We're members of the Sabbath School, every Sabbath Morning. This is the way we learn God's word, and all of His commandments. We need His word to fight the devil, who's trying to block our way. So come to Sabbath School, you will meet God there. Please be on time for your own soul's sake, for Jesus was never late.
Repeat

CHURCH ANTHEM

This is the church of the living God.
The pillar and ground of the truth,
The house of prayer for all people,
Commandment keepers are we.

We do not drink no wine,
We do not eat no swine.
We keep all the sayings of the Lord our God,
Commandment keepers are we.

We keep the Ten Commandments,
We keep the Sabbath too.
We keep all the feasts of the Lord our God,
Commandment keepers are we.

This is the church of the living God.
The pillar and ground of the truth,
The house of prayer for all people,
Commandment keepers are we.

SABBATH SONG

The seventh day is the Sabbath.
The seventh day is the Sabbath.
The seventh day is the Sabbath of the Lord.

The seventh day is the Sabbath.
The seventh day is the Sabbath.
The seventh day is the Sabbath of the Lord.

We do our washing on Sunday,
We do our ironing on Monday,
Tuesday and Wednesday, we work the same.
Clean our house on Thursday,
Shop a half day Friday,
Preparing for the Sabbath of the Lord.

The seventh day is the Sabbath.
The seventh day is the Sabbath.
The seventh day is the Sabbath of the Lord.

The seventh day is the Sabbath.
The seventh day is the Sabbath.
The seventh day is the Sabbath of the Lord.

CONTACT INFORMATION

General Headquarters
866 Georgetown Street
Lexington, KY 40511

Mailing Address
P.O. Box 13010
Lexington, KY 40583

Lock Box
P.O. Box 8081
Carol Stream, IL 60122
Cash App: $house866

Main Extension	859-252-4512
Apostle T.E. Clark, Jr.	859-967-2042
Apostle G.R. Dailey, Jr.	859-967-2031
General Secretary	859-967-2032
General Treasurer	859-967-2033

THE TWENTY-FOUR PRINCIPLES OF THE DOCTRINE OF JESUS CHRIST AND HIS APOSTLES

(Revised – 11/10/87)

1. **THE NEW BIRTH, YE MUST BE BORN AGAIN:** Jn. 3:1-7; I Jn. 3:9; Acts 2:1-4; II Cor. 5:17.
2. **THE KEEPING OF THE TEN COMMANDMENTS WRITTEN BY GOD'S OWN FINGER**: Ex. 20:1-17; Ex. 31:18; Ex. 32:15-16; Ecclesiastes 12:13; Jn. 14:15; Rev. 22:14-15.
3. **DIVINE HEALING:** Ex. 15:26; Isa. 53:4-5; Mark 9:23: Jn. 9:6-7.
4. **THE ADMINISTRATION OF FEET WASHING AND COMMUNION AT THE SAME SERVICE:** Jn. 13:4-17; Matt. 26:26-27; I Cor. 11:28-29
5. **TITHES AND OFFERINGS, AND EARLY DUTY OF THE PEOPLE OF GOD:** Gen. 28:22; Lev. 27:30-32; Matt. 23:23; Heb. 7:5.
6. **THE EATING OF SELECTIVE FOODS AS HOLY PEOPLE SHOULD:** Lev. 11:1-47; Deut. 14:1-21; Isa. 65:4-5, 66:17; Acts 15:20.
7. **EVERLASTING LIFE BEFORE GOING THROUGH THE GRAVE:** HOS. 13:14; JN. 3:16; I COR. 15:51; JN. 8:51.
8. **ABSOLUTE HOLINESS THROUGH THE LOVE OF GOD:** Jn. 13:34-35; II Cor. 7:1; Heb. 12:14; I Peter 1:15-16.
9. **RESURRECTION OF THE DEAD:** I Cor. 15:52; I Thess. 4:16; II Cor. 5:10; Rev. 20:13.
10. **THE TRANSLATION OF THE SAINTS**: Dan. 12:3; I Cor. 15:51; Phil. 3:21; I Jn. 3:2-3.

11. **THE SECOND COMING OF JESUS:** II Peter 3:10; Titus 2:13; Rev. 1:7, 22:16.
12. **THE THOUSAND YEARS, THE NEW HEAVEN, AND NEW EARTH:** Rev. 20:4-7; 21:1, II Peter 3:13.
13. **JESUS IS GOD, GOD IS JESUS:** Isa. 9:6, Luke 2:11, I Tim. 3:16; Jn. 1:13-14.
14. **BAPTIZE IN THE NAME OF JESUS CHRIST:** Acts 2:38; Gal. 3:27; Acts 4:10-12, 22:16.
15. **WATER ONLY FOR SACRAMENT:** Mark 9:41; Dan 1:12; Luke 22:20; John 19:34-35.
16. **WATER ALWAYS HAS BEEN USED FOR THE SALVATION WITH THE BLOOD:** Heb. 9:18-20; Num 19:13; I Jn 5:6-8; I Peter 3:20.
17. **SIN NOT AGAINST THE HOLY GHOST:** Matt. 12:31; Mark 3:28-29; Heb. 6:4-8, 10:26-31.
18. **ELECT AND ELECTION:** Isa. 45:4; Isa. 65:9; Matt. 24:22; Rom. 11:7.
19. **FOREKNOWLEDGE:** Jer. 1:5; Prov. 22:3; Rom. 11:2; I Peter 1:2-20.
20. **PRE-EXISTENCE OF JESUS:** Isa. 9:6; Micah 5:2; Jn. 8:58; Jn. 17:24.
21. **CHRIST REDEEMER ALWAYS:** Psa. 130:8; Hos. 13:14; Luke 1:68
22. **SIGNS:** Isa. 7:14; Ex. 4:8; Luke 2:12 ; Acts 2 :19.
23. **THE PASSOVER FOREVER, A TYPE OF CHRIST:** Ex. 12:24; I Peter 1:19; I Cor. 5:7-8.
24. **UNITY OF GOD'S PEOPLE:** Psa. 133:1; Psa. 81:11; Rom. 12:16; I Cor. 12:20.

Lesson F1 September 26, 2022
Ethanim 1, 5783

FEAST OF TRUMPETS

Introduction

On this first day of the seventh month, we celebrate a sabbath an holy convocation. A memorial; a day of blowing of trumpets. The trumpet was used for various purposes in the Scriptures. Prior to *Leviticus 23*, the trumpet was sounded in *Exodus 19* when the Lord came down to Mt Sinai. When the trump sounded long, it was a call to the people to come up to the mount. When the Lord descended upon the mount there were thunders and lightnings, and a thick cloud upon the mount, and the voice of the trumpet exceeding loud; so that all the people that were in the camp trembled.

Memory Verse *Ezekiel 33:4* Then whosoever heareth the sound of the trumpet, and taketh not warning; if the sword come, and take him away, his blood shall be upon his own head.

Biblical Application

At Mt. Sinai, the people were given specific direction by God through Moses. The penalty for failing follow the Lord's direction was death by stoning or being shot through. The Lord continued to warn and direct his people throughout the Old Testament using prophets. Their voices or writings were likened unto trumpets. Many times, the people refused to heed the warning of the Lord and suffered consequences for disobedience. From oppression, to captivity to death; the penalties were significant. God instructed Israel concerning the responsibility of watchmen through Ezekiel. The definition of the Hebrew word for watchman 6822 means to lean forward; to peer into the distance (Strong's Dictionary). When the Lord brought a sword upon a land; the watchman was to blow the trumpet, and warn the people. God gave specific warning through Ezekiel stating he had no pleasure in the death of the wicked and provided a way of escape. The New Testament contains numerous warnings from Jesus and the Apostles exhorting believers to holiness. As we celebrate this feast, let us take heed to the voice of trumpets.

- The watchman's trumpet. *Ezekiel 33: 1-20, Jeremiah 6:1,17.*
- Take heed to yourselves. *Luke 21:34-36; I Timothy 4:1-16; I Thessalonians 4:1-18.*
- Keep the feast with joy! *Numbers 29:1-6; Psalm 81:1-7.*

Everyday Life Application

How are you witnessing to those who are overcharged with surfeiting, and drunkenness, and cares of this life, and so that the day does not come upon them unaware as a snare?

Lesson 1 October 1, 2022
Ethanim 6, 5783

PERFECT PEACE

Introduction

Isaiah 25 and *26* prophesy of a future time when the Lord will swallow up death in victory and when dead men shall arise and live. We look with hope toward the time when this corruption shall put on incorruption and this mortal shall put on immortality (I Corinthians 15:54). *Isaiah 26* is a song that will be sung in Judah in that day. Even taken in its proper context; valuable principles are present in this song for us today. If our mind (framing, form, conception) is stayed (lean upon, take hold of) the Lord and trusteth (hide for refuge, attach oneself, confide in) he will keep us in perfect peace. The same Hebrew word for peace is used twice in this verse as perfect peace (safe, happy, welfare, health) (Strong's Dictionary)! The principle of peace found through trust in the Lord is present throughout the Scriptures.

Memory Verse *Isaiah 26:3* Thou wilt keep him in perfect peace, whose mind is stayed on thee: because he trusteth in thee.

Biblical Application

In *John 14,* after Jesus promised that the Comforter would come; he declared peace to his disciples. He said his peace was different from what the world gives. Peace of the world may result from favorable circumstances, economic prosperity, self-promotion or reliance, or simply the absence of war. Paul described the peace of God as passing all understanding and keeping our hearts and minds through Christ Jesus. This peace that Jesus and Paul talked about included instructions for us to maintain it. Jesus said to let not your heart be troubled (stir up) or afraid. Paul said to be careful(anxious) for nothing but instead by prayer and supplication with thanksgiving letting your requests be made known unto God (Strong's Dictionary). This means trusting the Lord in every situation and every circumstance. Even when things don't go how you wanted or expected you can have peace because you have the peace of God.

- Kept in perfect peace. *Isaiah 26: 1-12; John 14:26-27; Philippians 4:6-9; Psalm 37:11, 37, 119:165; Proverbs 3:2*
- There is no peace to the wicked. *Isaiah 48:18-22, 57:19-21.*
- The God of peace. *Romans 15:33; 16:20; II Corinthians 13:11, I Thessalonians 5:23, II Thessalonians 3:16.*

Everyday Life Application

Reflect on some of situations in your life that seemed to be full of chaos, but the Lord gave you peace. If you are lacking peace in your personal life, reevaluate your trust for Jesus.

Lesson F2 October 5, 2022
Ethanim 10, 5783

THE DAY OF ATONEMENT

Introduction

This 10th day of the 7th month is a holy convocation. Observance of this sabbath of rest includes afflicting your souls and doing no work at all. Strangers that sojourned among the children of Israel were also required to keep the feast. This day was observed once a year to make an atonement for the priest, his house, the children of Israel, the holy sanctuary, the tabernacle of the congregation, and for the altar.

Memory Verse *Leviticus 23:27* Also on the tenth day of this seventh month there shall be a day of atonement: it shall be an holy convocation unto you; and ye shall afflict your souls, and offer an offering made by fire unto the LORD.

Biblical Application

Observance of this feast was likely stressful to all those involved. The Lord was very specific on what he wanted done with the sacrifices and blood including their proper disposal. Adherence to details was crucial for the life of the priest. Prior to making any offerings, the priest had to wash with water then put on the holy linen garments. The high priest alone was allowed to enter within the vail where the mercy seat and ark of the covenant were located. He was required to offer sweet incense, enough to cover the mercy seat or die. Despite blood being shed and statutes fulfilled; this feast was imperfect at resolving the issue of sin. Even the daily offerings and sacrifices for sin were inadequate. They could not take away sin. Looking back to the original statutes should cause us to rejoice. We have joy in God through our Lord Jesus Christ, by whom we have now received the atonement (*Romans 5:11*). The death of Jesus Christ reconciled us to God. We have been justified by his blood and saved from wrath through him. While were yet sinners Christ died for us!

- Reconciled by his death. *Romans 5:1-11; Luke 7:36-50.*
- Rejoice in the Lord. *Philippians 4:4-9.*
- A holy convocation. *Numbers 29:7-11; Leviticus 16:1-34.*

Everyday Life Application

Reflect on the personal reconciliation the Jesus accomplished for you. Were you a debtor that owed fifty or five hundred pence?

Lesson 2 October 8, 2022
Ethanim 13, 5783

SHEW ME THY GLORY

Introduction

The hearing ear, and the seeing eye, the LORD hath made even both of them (*Proverbs 20:12*). As humans we relate to God and his creation primarily through hearing and sight. This lesson will focus on God's revelation through sight. Vision is the most complex, highly developed, and important sense to humans (Gerrig & Zimbardo)[1]. This makes placing faith in an invisible God an obstacle for many. However, God made all nations of men to dwell on the earth. He desires that they should seek the Lord, if haply they might feel after him, and find him, though he be not far from every one of us (Acts 17:26-27).

Memory Verse *Exodus 33:18* And he said, I beseech thee, shew me thy glory.

Biblical Application

As believers, we walk by faith and not by sight, but we all have an innate desire to see the glory of God (I *Corinthians 5:7)*. The angel of the Lord appeared to Moses in a flame of fire out of the midst of a bush. When he stopped to see the bush, God called to Moses. The Lord declared, I am the God of thy father, the God of Abraham, the God of Isaac, and the God of Jacob. Then Moses hid his face; for he was afraid to look upon God (*Exodus 3:4-6)*. The children of Israel experienced the glory of God through the visible cloud by day and the pillar of fire by night. In *Exodus 24: 17*, the sight of the glory of the Lord was like a devouring fire on the top of the mount. Later,

---

[1] Gerrig R. J., Zimbardo P. G. (2008). Psychology and Life, 18th Ed. Boston, MA: Pearson.

Moses beseeched the Lord to show him His glory. God declared that no man could see his face and live. He did allow Moses to see his back parts. There are other instances in the Scriptures when the Lord revealed some of his glory to man. When Isaiah saw the Lord sitting upon his throne; he was undone by his own unholiness. Smoke, fire, thunders, and lightings have all been associated with the appearance of the glory and presence of the Lord. Today, we see the glory of God in his creation and experience him through the Holy Spirit. The invisible things of him from the creation of the world are clearly seen, being understood by the things that are made, even his eternal power and Godhead (*Romans 1:20*). May the Lord continue to open our eyes to see the kingdom of God and to behold wonderous things out of his law. The Lord reveals himself to us in this life in a limited capacity; yet we stand in awe and reverence of the Almighty God!

- The invisible God. *I Timothy 1:17, 6:15-16; John 1:18; Romans 1:18-25.*
- Shew me thy glory. *Exodus 3: 1-6; 33:8-23.*
- The glory of God revealed. *Genesis 15:12-18, Exodus 19:16-21, 24:12-18, 40:38; Ezekiel 1:1-4, 26-28, 8:1-4; Isaiah 6:1-5, 66-15-19; Revelation 15:5-8.*

Everyday Life Application

How have you experienced the glory of God through the seeing eye?

Lesson F3 October 10, 2022
Ethanim 15, 5783

FEAST OF TABERNACLES

Introduction

Observance of the Lord's feasts were commanded beside (separate from) other sabbaths, gifts, vows, and freewill offerings. The Lord also commanded certain offerings to be made by fire on his feast days. They included a burnt offering, a meat offering, a sacrifice, and drink offerings. Entire households were to rejoice in the feast. This included thou, and thy son, and thy daughter, and thy manservant, and thy maidservant, and the Levite, the stranger, and the fatherless, and the widow, that are within thy gates. We celebrate (march in a procession) this solemn feast because the Lord has blessed us in all our increase, and in all the works of our hands, therefore we surely rejoice.

Memory Verse *Leviticus 23:38* Beside the sabbaths of the LORD, and beside your gifts, and beside all your vows, and beside all your freewill offerings, which ye give unto the LORD.

Biblical Application

Today we proclaim (call out) this holy (set apart) convocation (rest) according to the Scriptures (Strong's Dictionary). Let us to make an offering and sacrifice unto the Lord for his blessings to us. The blessings of God are apparent in our lives. He has provided a source of income, various types of food, means of transportation, a place of shelter with modern amenities, a certain degree of health, the presence of family, friends, and the fellowship of the saints. These are just a few of the Lord's blessings to us. Proclaiming the feasts of Lord includes explaining the relevancy of the Lord's feasts to believers today. The world is unashamed in promotion of their most celebrated events and holidays with pagan traditions. When others speak to you of holidays such as Christmas or Easter, it opens a door of opportunity to speak about the Lord's feasts. This feast points prophetically to the thousand-year reign of Christ and will be observed in the future. Let us not be ashamed to proclaim the gospel of Jesus Christ including the feast days.

- Proclaim the Lord's feasts. *Leviticus 23:37-38; Psalm 145:1-21, Romans 1:16-17.*
- The feast will be kept in the future. *Zechariah 14:16-19.*
- Observe the feast. *Deuteronomy 16:13-17.*

Everyday Life Application

What is the Lord requiring of you for his kingdom besides not practicing sin? Are there sacrifices and offerings the Lord has asked of you personally?

Lesson 3 October 15, 2022
Ethanim 20, 5783

GOOD WORKS

Introduction

America is one of the richest nations on earth, yet there are people who are food insecure or hungry living in our communities. There are people and entire families who are homeless or lack permanent housing. Some individuals are forced to cut-back on groceries in order to afford medications. Our government assists those who qualify, but sometimes, it is not enough and there is still some lack of food, money for housing or medication. As Christians, we are required to do good works, and as we are able, we should help men, women and children in need of assistance. While teaching the disciples, Jesus said, "Let your light so shine before men, that they may see your good works, and glorify your Father which is in heaven." When we do good works, God is glorified.

Memory Verse *Titus 2:14 Who* gave himself for us, that he might redeem us from all iniquity, and purify unto himself a peculiar people, zealous of good works.

Biblical Application

Good is defined as morally right or righteous. Works in the Greek (Strong's G2041) is translated as ergon which means deeds, actions, labor or anything we do. Good works are deeds or actions that are morally right or righteous. They are not done for attention. We should be careful not to announce that we are doing good works. Good deeds should be done out of our love for God and never any selfish motive. As Christians, we were created in Christ Jesus unto good works. While our works do not save us, good works are required. Christ did good works and so did the disciples, and we are to follow their example. This lesson reminds us to do and maintain good works and glorify God.

- We are created to do good works and be zealous. *Ephesians 2:8-10; Titus 2:11-14.*
- Biblical examples of good works. *Matthew 25:35-40, 26:6-12; I Timothy 6:17-19.*
- God is glorified through good works. *Matthew 5:16; I Peter 2:12.*
- Take heed when doing good works. *Matthew 6:1-4*
- Good works should be fruitful and be maintained. *Colossians 1:7-10; Titus 3:14.*
- We will be rewarded according to our works. *Revelation 22:12.*

Everyday Life Application

Are you feeding the hungry, visiting the sick, or helping provide clothes to people or families who need them? There are many ways to reach those who need assistance. Please share the opportunities available in your community to help those in need.

Author: Minister Sophia Eaves

Lesson F4 October 17, 2022
Ethanim 22, 5783

FEAST OF TABERNACLES LAST GREAT DAY

Introduction

We celebrate this eighth day, a holy convocation unto the Lord. This feast was one of the three times a year in which the Lord made certain requirements for males. They were commanded to appear before the Lord which means to see the face or to turn to face and see the Lord in the place he chose (selected). This required deliberate and purposeful action. Males were not to appear before the Lord empty (ineffectually, without cause) and were supposed to give as able (present a sacrificial offering with an open hand) according to the blessing which the Lord gave them (Strong's Dictionary).

Memory Verse *Deuteronomy 16:16* Three times in a year shall all thy males appear before the LORD thy God in the place which he shall choose; in the feast of unleavened bread, and in the feast of weeks, and in the feast of tabernacles: and they shall not appear before the LORD empty.

Biblical Application

The Lord placed the responsibility upon man to be the leader of his family. This does not make women or other family members less important or less significant. The Lord gave specific instructions to man concerning demonstration of love and respect towards women and children. The man has a duty and accountability to lead his family to follow the commandments of the Lord. Thus, men were commanded to turn to face and see the Lord in three feasts each year. The Lord commanded that his word be taught diligently unto children, and be talked of when sitting in thine house, and when walking by the way, and when lying down, and when thou risest up.

This was so when the Lord gave them great and goodly cities, houses full of all good things, wells, vineyards and olive trees, when they had eaten and were full, then beware lest thou forget the LORD. As we rejoice and enjoy the blessings of God let us remain diligent in his Word looking unto the fulfillment of this last great day at the new heavens and new earth.

- Love the Lord and teach thy children diligently. *Deuteronomy 6:1-15.*
- Appear before the Lord. *Exodus 23:14-1; Deuteronomy 16:13-17.*
- Lead with love and respect. *Ephesians 5:22-33, 6:1-4.*

Everyday Life Application

How did you prepare to see the face or appear before the Lord at this feast? How can you improve your leadership amongst your family into the ways of Christ?

Lesson 4 October 22, 2022
Ethanim 27. 5783

A PROPER RESPONSE

Introduction

In *John 16:33*, Jesus lets us know that in this life we shall have tribulation, which points to seasons of intense pressure, whether literally or figuratively. As believers, this is a reality that we have to be mindful of. Not only are tribulations a part of our experience, but struggles, hardships, trials, persecutions and temptations are a part as well. The challenge for us when these things come upon us, no matter how much pain we feel, no matter how much our flesh want to lash out, is to have a proper response. Our response to people and to God matters. We don't want to be guilty of lashing out at people (when they are the source of our negative experience) and or charging God foolishly because He has allowed the situation.

Memory Verse: *I Thessalonians 5:18* In everything give thanks: for this is the will of God in Christ Jesus concerning you.

Biblical Application

Romans 15:4 points to the fact that Scriptures were written aforetime for our learning that we through the patience and comfort of the scripture would have hope. As we look at Israel in the wilderness, we can learn from them the perils of not having the right responses. God was grieved with them *(Hebrew 3:8-10*) because their response to temptation was almost always wrong, and full of accusations, murmuring and complaining *(Exodus 16:1-8; Numbers 14:1-3.)* As a result of their wrong, response, they missed out on the promise God had in store for them. In contrast to Israel, when we have a proper response, it's not suggesting that there is an absence of pain, frustration, emotion, or suffering, but it points to a level of faith and trust in God; it points to a recognition of future blessing and glory. A proper response is full if rejoicing, thanksgiving and worship. This lesson is designed to encourage us to grow in the area of our response.

- Proper response. *Matthew 5:10-12; James 1:2-4; I Peter 4:12-14.*
- Believer's example ship. *Job 1:20-22; Acts 5:18-41.*
- Response to our perpetrators. *Matthew 5:44-48; Romans 12:14-21.*

Everyday Life Application

Discuss seasons you've endured intense tribulation, persecution, etc. How did you handle it? Was your response proper or improper?

Author: Elder James Taylor, Jr.

Lesson 5 October 29, 2022
Bul 4, 5783

AS NEWBORN BABES

Introduction

In the closing verses of *I Peter 1*, we are exhorted to love one another with a pure heart fervently. A comparison is then given between the eternal Word of God and frailty of human flesh. This flesh or grass is withering or aging and the glory or flower of it is falling away. God's word will stand forever. Accordingly, Peter then admonishes us of certain things we must put off completely. These include malice (malignity), guile (trickery), hypocrisies (deceit), envies (ill will), and evil speaking (defamation) (Strong's Dictionary).

Memory Verse *I Peter 2:2* As newborn babes, desire the sincere milk of the word, that ye may grow thereby.

Biblical Application

After directing us to put off all these things, the Scriptures provide us clear direction as believers. We are exhorted to become as newborn babies and to desire (intensely crave possession) the sincere (unadulterated, undeceitful) milk of the word. According to the CDC, newborn babies should eat at least every 2-4 hours.[2] It may even be necessary to wake a baby from sleep to feed them in order to ensure proper nutrition. Babies grow at impressive rates; on average they grow ½ to 1 inch a month. By 5 months of age, they should double their birth weight and by one year triple their birth weight (Mayo Clinic). This admonition is pushing us to do much more than listen to the preached word on Sabbath Day or read the Word once a week. The Bible is admonishing us to have

[2] https://www.cdc.gov/nutrition/infantandtoddlernutrition

https://www.mayoclinic.org/healthy-lifestyle/infant-and-toddler-health

frequent, intense cravings for the unadulterated Word. The word sincere is deliberate in its push to let the Word speak to us as God's intended. This is apart from our personal interpretation and that of false teachers. If we want to grow spiritually, we have to eat the sincere milk of God's Word every day. In order to observe to do according to all that is written in the book of the law, we must not let it depart from our mouth, but meditate in it day and night. If we practice mediation (murmur, ponder, mutter) on God's law and do all that is written therein; we are promised prosperous ways and good success (Strong's Dictionary).

- Become as a newborn babe. *I Peter 1:22-25, 2:1-10; Job 23:11-12.*
- Meditate day and night and do. *Joshua 1:6-9; Psalm 119: 9-16; James 1:21-25.*
- Lay up the Word in your heart and soul. *Deuteronomy 11:18-25; 6:4-9.*

Everyday Life Application

What is the spiritual application of binding the Word as a sign upon thine hand, being as frontlets between thine eyes, writing them on your posts and gate?

Lesson 6 November 5, 2022
Bul 11, 5783

THE CHOSEN FAST

Introduction

In the Old Testament, fasting (abstaining from food and drink), along with prayer, were used to entreat God for a specific concern or matter. In scripture, Jehoshaphat proclaimed a fast when the Moabites and Ammonites came against Israel. David fasted so that his child, born of Bathsheba, would live; and Esther had her people fast before she prepared to go before the King to save Israel. In all these examples, fasting and prayer were used to seek God's divine intervention. Isaiah chapter 58 opens with God telling the Prophet Isaiah to cry loud and spare not and to show Israel their transgressions and sins. Israel desires to know why God does not see and acknowledge their fasting. God states that Israel seeks him daily, and delight to know his ways, but they are as a nation that did righteousness and did not forsake His ordnances. God exposes Israel's sin and reveals what deeds and acts of compassion are most important to Him. This lesson aims to teach us what God considers as an acceptable fast.

Memory Verse *Isaiah 58:6* Is not this the fast that I have chosen? to loose the bands of wickedness, to undo the heavy burdens, and to let the oppressed go free, and that ye break every yoke?

Biblical Application

During fasting, God's people turned their attention to God, and they prayed and believed that God would respond to their most urgent requests. In Isaiah 58, God exposes Israel's true motivation of the fast, which was for strife, debate and to inflict injury on others. God establishes the kind of fast He finds acceptable. We learn that we must love others, show compassion, give to the needy and care for our families. Our times of fasting and prayer should be centered on God. God shows us how our motives and acts of compassion (not our fasting) are directly related to him hearing us and blessing us.

- During fasting and prayer, our hearts and minds are only toward God. *Isaiah 58:4; Joel 1:14; 2:12; Matthew 6:16-18.*
- We must loose bands of wickedness and set the oppressed free. *Deuteronomy 24:14; Isaiah 58:4-6; Proverbs 3:3-4, 11:17; Micah 6:8.*
- Have compassion and show kindness. *Deuteronomy 15:7-8; Isaiah 58:7, 10; Matthew 25:31-40; Luke 10:25-37.*
- When we follow God's guidance, he responds and blesses us. *Isaiah 58:8-12.*

Everyday Life Application

God is concerned about how we treat others and how we take care of those in need. Are you living a life that demonstrates compassion and kindness toward others? How do you personally help those who in need? How might your church organize to help those in need? Please feel free to share.

Author: Minister Sophia Eaves

Lesson 7 November 12, 2022
Bul 18, 5783

EFFECTIVE COMMUNICATION

Introduction

Have you ever been in the presence of a master communicator? You hang on for their next word, they can connect with you and their passion and conviction are evident in the words they speak. Can you imagine being at the March on Washington when Dr. Martin Luther King Jr so eloquently gave our country a glimpse into his dream. Other examples are when the Apostle Paul stood before King Agrippa and at the end of his appeal, King Agrippa shares almost thou persuadest me to be a Christian *(Acts 26:28),* or Peter as he stood up at the Day of Pentecost and spoke so boldly that men ask, what must we do? *(Acts 2:37)* These are all great examples of communication to large audiences. However, most of our communication occurs with smaller groups or one on one and it is essential we can communicate effectively. Some researchers believe more than 90% of our communication is nonverbal which means not involving words or speech. Our body language, eye contact and facial expressions can have a major influence on how people receive our message.

Memory Verse *Psalms 19:14* Let the words of my mouth, and the mediation of my heart, be acceptable in thy sight, O Lord, my strength, and my redeemer.

Biblical Application

Effective communication is a critical skill both in and outside of the church. As believers what we say may be true, but we must be mindful we have the right tone, attitude, and communicate with love. What I say to a person may be correct and well-intended, however, the message may not be received because of my delivery. It is not what you say but how you say it. Our words matter and have power. We often quote the scripture, death and life are in the power of the tongue: and they that love it shall eat the fruit thereof (*Proverbs 18:21)*; however, do we fully understand we must be mindful of the words we speak? Pastor Rick Warren states, you are never persuasive when you are abrasive, and you never get your point across by being cross.

- Guard your mouth. *Ephesians 4:29-31* [Explore the text: How does grieving the spirit tie into our communication?], *Colossians 4:5-6, Psalms 141:3.*
- How we respond to people is a part of our communication. *Proverbs 15:1-4.*
- One of the greatest skills to develop to be an effective communicator is to be a good and active listener. *James 1:19; Proverbs 19:20, 18:13.*

Everyday Life Application

What is one thing you believe you can work on to become a more effective communicator?

Author: Deacon Walter H. Preston, Jr.

Lesson 8 November 19, 2022
Bul 25, 5783

BE CAREFUL FOR NOTHING

Introduction

In *Judges 6,* the Lord delivered Israel into the hands of the Midianites for seven years because of their sins. The Midianites and the Amalekites destroyed their crops to the point where there was no sustenance for the people or their livestock. Israel was greatly impoverished and forced to live in caves in the mountains. When the people cried to the Lord, he was clear about their disobedience in serving other gods.

Memory Verse *Philippians 4:6.* Be careful for nothing; but in everything by prayer and supplication with thanksgiving let your requests be made known unto God.

Biblical Application

Gideon was well acquainted with the oppression of the Midianites. He was secretly threshing wheat at the winepress when the Lord called him. Gideon did not immediately respond with strong faith. In fact, Gideon expressed doubt and anxiety to the Lord on more than one occasion. He heard about the miracles God performed in Egypt, but now asked a question that had likely lingered with him for years. "If the Lord be with us then why is this befallen us?" Gideon went on to question the Lord further and ask for signs from the Lord. God knew his character and chose him anyway. The Lord even told him to take his servant with him to calm his fear when he went to the Midianite camp. After overcoming his struggle with fear, Gideon demonstrated great faith and was used by God to deliver Israel from the Midianites. The Bible contains various examples of flawed individuals like Moses, Gideon, Thomas, and Simon Peter who struggle with doubt, anxiety, and fear; but are able to overcome. Let us be careful (anxious) for nothing; but communicate to God openly and honestly in everything; casting all your cares upon Him for he careth for you.

- The Lord is our peace. *Judges 6: 11-24.*
- Gideon expresses his doubt and fear. *Judges 6:25-27, 36-40, 7:9-14.*
- Cast all your care upon him. *I Peter 5:6-9; Philippians 4:4-7; Proverbs 3:5-6; Matthew 6:25-34.*

Everyday Life Application

How do you express your human emotions to God? Does prayer or praise provide an outlet of communication with God for you?

Lesson 9 November 26, 2022
Kislev 2, 5783

DO GOOD UNTO ALL MEN

Introduction

Galatians 6: 6-10 begins with instruction concerning giving to those who teach the Word. Then the law of reaping and sowing addresses sowing to the flesh or the Spirit. Finally, we are told to do good unto all men especially(particularly) the household of faith (Strong's Dictionary). The Bible gives consistent guidance concerning doing good unto all men. The royal law according to *James 2*:8 is to love thy neighbor as thyself. Jesus also made it clear that the law and the prophets were instruct us to do unto others as you would have done to you.

Memory Verse *Galatians 6:10* As we have therefore opportunity, let us do good unto all men, especially unto them who are of the household of faith.

Biblical Application

The Bible provides instructions about how the people of God should handle money and conduct business. Usury in Hebrew is interest on a debt and comes from a root word meaning to strike with a sting or oppress with interest (Strong's Dictionary). Our society abounds with unjust business practices such as predatory lenders and exorbitant banking fees that prey on the poor. Saints must be careful not to engage in unjust business practices with anyone, especially believers. In *Nehemiah 5*, the people of God were working to rebuild Jerusalem. There was a dearth in the land and some had mortgaged lands, vineyards and houses to buy corn. Some had borrowed for the king's tribute. The nobles and rulers were oppressing their own brethren with usury. They took advantage of the poverty of the in order to make maximal profits. This injustice made Nehemiah was very angry and motivated him to take action. The willingness to oppress others resulted from a lack of fear of God. As believers, our fear of God and faith in his Word becomes apparent in our personal business practices and those we engage in at work.

- Do good unto all men. *Galatians 6:6-10; Matthew 7:12-14.*
- Avoid oppressing any. *Ezekiel 18:4-5, 7-10, 12-14, 17-18; Exodus 22:25; Deuteronomy 23:19-20; Psalm 15:5; Proverbs 28:8.*
- Walk in the fear of God. *Nehemiah 5:1-13.*

Everyday Life Application

If your employer engages in unrighteous business practices, should you engage because it is part of your job? Pray about ways you should do good to the household of faith.

Lesson 10 December 3, 2022
Kislev 9, 5783

FROM HURT TO HEALED

Introduction

The concept of personal relationship is almost as old as time itself. In *Genesis 2:18*, God said "It is not good that the man should be alone; I will make him an help meet for him." God blessed us with the opportunity to build relationships with others. In His infinite wisdom, He also gave us clear instructions on how to treat each other with love. But what happens when someone fails to follow those instructions and that offense leads to emotional hurt? How do you move from being hurt to being healed?

Memory Verse *Jeremiah 17:14 Heal* me, O Lord, and I shall be healed; save me, and I shall be saved: for thou art my praise.

Biblical Application

Genesis chapters 37, 39 - 45 records the history of Joseph. His brothers sold him into slavery. Afterwards, he was sexually harassed, accused of rape, and thrown into prison. But in chapter 45, Joseph teaches a powerful lesson about forgiveness. He said to his brothers, "Come near to me, I pray you. And they came near. And he said, I am Joseph your brother, whom ye sold into Egypt. Now therefore be not grieved, nor angry with yourselves, that ye sold me hither: for God did send me before you to preserve life" (*Genesis 45:4-5*). Joseph could have taken revenge against his brothers, but he was more focused on forgiveness. He could have dwelt on past hurts, but he was more preoccupied with preservation of life.

[3] "Overcoming Bitterness: Moving from Life's Greatest Hurts to a Life Filled with Joy."

Stephen Viars, Baker Books, 2021. ISBN 1493428837, 9781493428830

Unrestrained bitterness is destructive (Viars, 2021)[3]. However, there is great power in moving past the hurt. You don't have to be burdened by bitterness. You can choose to be healed. You can choose to be happy!

- Forgiveness is essential. *Mark 11:25; Matthew 6:15.*
- Get rid of the bitterness. *Ephesians 4:31-32; Hebrews 12:14-15.*
- Ask God to heal your heart. *Psalm 51:10; Psalm 147:3; Jeremiah 17:14.*

Everyday Life Application

Forgiving others and letting go of bitterness can often be difficult. Moving from being hurt to being healed may not happen overnight. However, both are not only possible but also necessary for our own health and wellbeing. If you are struggling with past hurts, ask God to help you overcome the spirit of heaviness. We can do all things through Christ who strengthens us.

Author: Deacon James Fant, Jr.

Lesson 11 December 10, 2022
Kislev 16, 5783

GOD IS ABLE

Introduction

Throughout the Bible, there are examples of gifts, offerings, and sacrifices given by people to the Lord. As Creator, the Lord owns all things. He has entrusted some of those things to us in a stewardship. Unfortunately, giving towards the work of God is often misunderstood or misrepresented. Churches and charities use various methods to solicit financial gifts. Some methods involve touching emotions, while others make promises for blessings and healing, which they are unable to provide. As good stewards we have a responsibility to use wisdom in our giving.

Memory Verse *II Corinthians 9:8* And God is able to make all grace abound toward you; that ye, always having all sufficiency in all things, may abound to every good work:

Biblical Application

II Corinthians 9 provides insights into sound giving. The church was zealous and ready to give to the ministering (aid, service) to the saints. This was to supply the want of the saints and resulted in many thanksgivings to God. Verse 6 reiterates what Jesus said in *Luke 6:38*. If we sow sparingly, we will reap sparingly; we will receive based on the measure that we mete. This is the opposite to the covetousness or greed practiced by the world which focuses on reaping and maximizing profits at the expense of people. Our giving should not be grudgingly (origin of sadness) or of necessity (constraint, distress), but cheerfully. The ability of God to make all grace abound toward us should motivate us to give. This results in always having all sufficiency (contentedness, competence, self-satisfaction) in all things and increase in every good work. The promise here goes far beyond financial blessings. As it does in

Malachi 3. God said to prove (test, investigate) him by giving tithes and offerings. The Lord promises to pour you out a blessing that you will not have room enough to receive it. This includes rebuking the devourer (consume, burn up) and preventing the vine from casting her fruit early(miscarry) (Strong's Dictionary). The blessing of God will be apparent on our lives, others will call you blessed and a delightsome land. Let our giving be based on God's promises and not the words or actions of others.

- The law of sowing and reaping. *II Corinthians 9:1-15*; *Luke 6:30-38*.
- Fear the Lord. *Psalm 112:1-10; Malachi 3:6-12*.
- Don't err from the faith. *I Timothy 6:1-10 Acts 20:33-35*.

Everyday Life Application

How have you seen giving misrepresented in the church? Thank God for all the devourers that He has rebuked from your life. This includes health, employment, school, family, etc.

Lesson 12 December 17, 2022
Kislev 23, 5783

IN HIM WILL I TRUST

Introduction

Psalm 91 has been used as a prayer by many over the centuries. Although the author is not listed in the Bible; the message is powerful. When applying the verses to our personal lives, we must consider the entire Psalm. Unfortunately, the adversary continues to use people today to isolate and misinterpret verses of Scripture out of context to lie about the character of the Lord. Some have misused certain verses in this Psalm to think they can act haphazardly; quote a verse or two and get instantaneous miraculous deliverance. In our next lesson, we will examine how Satan used verses from Psalm 91 to tempt Jesus.

Memory Verse *Psalm 91:2* I will say of the LORD, He is my refuge and my fortress: my God; in him will I trust.

Biblical Application

Psalm 91 provides details about what it means to have a close relationship with the Lord. The psalmist makes deliberate decisions to draw close to God and reaps numerous benefits as a result. The writer begins by speaking of those that dwell (to sit down, settle) with the Almighty and abide (stay permanently under his shadow(defense). He declares the Lord is his refuge(shelter) and fortress(fastness) and the writer trusts in Him. This closeness results in deliverance from the fowler (trapper) and pestilence(plague). The cover of God's wings and surrounding of his shield and buckler ensures there is no need to fear what may come during the day or night. Making God a refuge and habitation (abode, asylum) results in several benefits (Strong's Dictionary). Protection from evil, plagues, and the protection of angels are a few. This deliverance is not absolute immunity from trouble but a reassurance of deliverance when trouble occurs. Trusting in the Lord and remaining close to him results in protection and deliverance from numerous dangers both seen and unseen by the natural eye.

- Choose to draw close and trust in the Lord. *Psalm 91:1-4; James 4:1-10.*
- Benefits of trusting Him. *Psalm 91:5-8; 145:17-21.*
- Make the Lord thy habitation and love Him. *Psalm 91: 9-16; II Samuel 22:1-20.*

Everyday Life Application

Have you prayed or quoted God's Word over your life and seen results? Deacon Oliver Mabson Sr. testified about *Psalm 91* when he was a soldier in the Korean War. At the direction of one of the saints, he prayed this Psalm every day and made it home alive!

Lesson 13 December 24, 2022
Kislev 30, 5783

THE NEED FOR THE APOLOGIST

Introduction
In this age of information in which we live, we (mankind) have access to more material than we could ever process. The information available covers every possible subject that man can imagine. With the spirit of anti-Christ in the earth, the study of philosophies and religions that support the spirit of antichrist in the earth should raise major concerns. The reasoning being the information in these two fields are in direct opposition of the teachings of the one true God. In addition, the infallibility of the Holy Scriptures is often challenged and because of the pseudo-scholarship being used, many claim plagiarism. As a result of these false claims against YHWH and the Holy Scriptures, thousands have not come to the faith, or have turned their back on what they once believed. Apologist are needed to combat this false messaging. Webster's Dictionary defines an apologist as one who speaks or writes in defense of someone or something. And the apologist, throughout the centuries have had major effectiveness in the defending and advancement of God's kingdom message.

Memory Verse *I Peter 3:15* But sanctify the Lord God in your hearts: and be ready always to give an answer to every man that asketh you a reason of the hope that is in you with meekness and fear:

Biblical Application

To be an effective apologist, we must possess at least some of the following characteristics: conviction, personal experience, knowledge and understanding of the Scripture; the leading of the Holy Spirit, a level of understanding of other teachings and their origins. A point that we need to establish is not every apologist is meant to tackle areas of philosophies and/or other religions. Some apologists are meant to defend the faith internally and combat the false teaching of the scriptures in the body of Christ. To some degree, every true believer of God has the capacity and qualifications to be an apologist. One should never underestimate the power, and effectiveness of a personal testimony, as a defense of the faith.

- Peter & the Apostles. *Acts 5:16-33, 2:14-40.*
- Paul. *Acts 17:22-31, 22:1-2, 26:1-23.*
- Philip. *Acts 8:5-13.*
- Defending our common salvation. *Jude: 3-19.*

Everyday Life Application

Testify to moment you've had to defend the faith, whether it was against a different religion., or whether you defended pure church doctrine.

- Materials that defend the bible:
- In the beginning (Walt Brown)
- A case for Christ (Lee Strobel
- The book of Josephus
- Mere Christian. (C S. Lewis)
- I don't have enough faith to be atheist (Geisler & Turek)
- Kent Hovind, creation series
- Gods Not Dead, the movie

Author: Elder James Taylor, Jr.

Lesson 14 December 31, 2022
Tebeth 7, 5783

MAKE TO YOURSELVES FRIENDS

Introduction

The Lord put man in the garden of Eden to dress it and to keep it (*Genesis 2:15)*. God expects us to accomplish work and has blessed each of us with talents and abilities to do so. In *Luke 16*, Jesus told a parable to his disciples about a steward. A steward may be an employee, overseer, manager, house distributor, treasurer, or fiscal agent (Strong's Dictionary). This parable has been misunderstood by some since the time it was spoken. The Pharisees heard the parable and derided Jesus after he spoke it. Jesus reproved the covetous Pharisees, because in their hearts they cared about the money or goods and missed the point. Others have attempted to use the parable to justify dishonesty in business.

Memory Verse *Luke 16:9* And I say unto you, ~~Make~~make to yourselves friends of the mammon of unrighteousness; that, when ye fail, they may receive you into everlasting habitations.

Biblical Application

The steward of a rich man was accused of wasting his lord's goods. The steward was told that he was about to lose his job and made preparation. His position gave him an opportunity to be able to adjust the bills of those who owed the ruler. The adjustments saved the debtors money and gave him favor in their sight. The purpose of adjusting their bills was to have a place to go when he lost his job. He built a relationship with the debtors by acting on their behalf. Jesus referred to him as the unjust steward and said the lord commended him for his wisdom. The children of this world are wiser than the children of light in their ability to make friends of the mammon (wealth or confidence) of unrighteousness. As children of light, we need to build relationships at work, in business, at school, at church and in the community that can benefit us when a need arises. Jesus was not justifying the unjust steward's unfaithfulness or crooked business practices. This is clear in verses 10-13 when he states we must be faithful in the least and no servant can serve two masters. We cannot serve God and mammon, but we need to use wisdom to make friends and build relationships.

- The parable of the steward. *Luke 16:1-15.*
- Stewards must be faithful. *I Corinthians 4:1-2; Proverbs 11:1, 16:11, 20:10-23; Leviticus 19:13, 33-37; Deuteronomy 8:11-20.*
- Build healthy relationships. *Matthew 7:12; Romans 12:9-18; Proverbs 17:17, 18:24.*

Everyday Life Application

How can you improve your professional relationships to make friends of the mammon of unrighteousness? Expand this list of attributes of faithful stewards: honest, hardworking, punctual, competent, and professional.

Lesson 15 January 7, 2023
Tebeth 14, 5783

LORD, I NEED YOUR HELP

Introduction

Over the last few years, there have been things that have impacted our world collectively and individually. We have experienced social unrest with the deaths of George Floyd, Brianna Taylor and there are many more. The Covid 19 pandemic has claimed millions of lives. Political division has turned into tribalism and divided us into red or blue camps. There is an appearance of the lack of civility in our political discourse and interaction to divide and separate us. As inflation skyrockets, the war in Ukraine and a looming recession, it is easy to simply lose hope, become discouraged and overwhelmed. It is a blessing to know Jesus Christ and have a personal relationship with him. However, we live in the natural world and must face the realities and circumstances of life. Our mental and emotional well-being are essential for us to have balanced lives. It is okay to not be okay and we must learn how to ask for help. We are never intended to go through life as a lone ranger, on solo missions believing we can endure anything by ourselves. As Hezekiah Walker states in his song, I need you to survive, I need you and you need me, we are all a part of God's body.

Memory Verse *Psalms 61:1-2* Hear my cry, O God; attend unto my prayer. From the end of the earth will I cry unto thee, when my heart is overwhelmed: lead me to the rock that is higher than I.

Biblical Application

I believe people can relate to the stories about the psalmist David when he would pour out his soul to God. We hear accounts of his high and low points. We see his remarkable success in battle, how he united Israel and him dancing as he brings the Ark of the Covenant to Jerusalem. We also see his low moments as he commits adultery with Bathsheba and has her husband Uriah killed, the death of some of his children and his disobedience. Just like with David, we have our highs and our lows and sometimes life itself can be overwhelming. If we are honest with ourselves, we can become discouraged, disappointed, and simply want to give up. We experience a sudden loss and wonder why? We get a bad doctor's report and struggle to figure out what is next? Be confident in this, no matter what, you are not alone. Do not lose hope, keep the faith, and realize God will support, shelter, and sustain you during the storms of life. We must learn it is okay to ask for help not only from God, our church family, and other believers. We can also get help by seeking out and engaging with licensed and professionally trained therapist. Getting therapy can be great for our mental and emotional well-being.

- We as believers are helpers one to another. *Galatians 6:1-3.*
- We need the help and support of others. *Ecclesiastes 4:9-12.*
- God will not forsake us. *Deuteronomy 31:1-8, Hebrews 13:5-6.*
- It is okay to ask for help. Mark 9:23-27.

Everyday Life Application

When life overwhelms you, how do you relieve stress? How do you ask for help when you are struggling mentally or emotionally?

Author: Deacon Walter H. Preston, Jr.

Lesson 16 January 14, 2022
Tebeth 21, 5783

OWE NO MAN ANYTHING

Introduction

As of the 3rd quarter of 2021, the two largest categories of U.S. household debt continued to rise. The total U.S. student loan debt was $1.58 trillion and the total mortgage debt was $10.67 trillion (NYFED)[4]. Many in the church have taken on one or both of these types of debt. Both have potential for a good return on investment. Care must be taken to ensure student loan debt is for a field that has demand for workers and provides enough income for repayment. This lesson will explore some of what the Bible says concerning debts.

Memory Verse *Romans 13:8* Owe no man anything, but to love one another: for he that loveth another hath fulfilled the law.

Biblical Application

Romans 13:6-8 provides practical financial advice to pay tribute (taxes) and dues(indebtedness). As the people of God, we must be careful to be honest in our financial affairs. Committing tax fraud or defaulting on loans does not glorify God. One of the most sobering verses concerning loans says the borrower is servant to the lender (*Proverbs 22:7*). Once you sign the loan papers and receive the disbursement then you become a servant to that person or institution. Care should be taken to negotiate and examine the terms of loans. Part of the negotiation involves maintaining good credit and avoidance of unnecessary debt. It is important to ensure that your credit report is correct and to fix previous financial missteps. A difference of 1% interest on a 30-year fixed rate home mortgage translates into thousands or tens of thousands of dollars

---

[4] https://www.newyorkfed.org/newsevents/news/research/2021/20211109

over the term of the loan. Be willing to follow a budget and take steps such as paying extra towards the principal each month. Caution is advised against being a surety (be security) or cosigning for others debts (Strong's Dictionary). Cosigners are often required for those who are higher risk for default. Let us take care to be diligent in business in order to stand before kings and not mean men (*Proverbs 22:29*).

- Practical financial advice. *Romans 13:1-8; Proverbs 22:7.*
- Avoid being a surety. *Proverbs 6:1-5, 11:15, 17:18, 22:26-27.*
- Be diligent in business. *Proverbs 10:4-5, 12:11, 22:29.*

Everyday Life Application

Assess how you can improve your current financial situation. What steps are you taking to avoid being servant to the lender?

Lesson 17 January 21, 2023
Tebeth 28, 5783

A MORE EXCELLENT WAY

Introduction

Apostle Paul, writes a beautiful letter to the church at Corinth encouraging, correcting and teaching the saints. He addresses issues of the day such as divisions in the church, sexual immorality, marriage, idolatry, head coverings, and more. In *I Corinthians 12,* Paul discusses spiritual gifts and ministries. He teaches that spiritual gifts are imparted to those who have the Holy Spirit, and that these spiritual gifts benefit the church. In the latter part of *I Corinthians 12,* Paul uses the metaphor of the body to explain how the saints are Christ's body and are many members within the body. He goes further and reidentifies the spiritual gifts and ministries and encourages the saints to "covet earnestly" or desire the best gifts. Apostle Paul ends the chapter by suggesting a more excellent way than desiring the best spiritual gifts.

Memory Verse *I Corinthians 12:31 But* covet earnestly the best gifts: and yet shew I unto you a more excellent way.

Biblical Application

While spiritual gifts can be desired and are needed in the church, Paul strongly teaches that charity or love is most important. Common usage of the word love means an intense feeling of deep affection. The word charity as found in *I Corinthians 13:1* is translated from the Greek word agape (Strong's G26) which means affection or benevolence. Also, charity is defined as love, benevolence or good will. Apostle Paul encourages the saints to have charity. When we don't have love, we are nothing. Although we may perform altruistic acts, it profits us nothing. Today, we are reminded that as saints we are required to love.

- Love is a more excellent way. *I Corinthians 13*
- Love is proof of discipleship. *John 13:34-35*
- Love should be fervent. *I Peter 4:8*
- God is love. *I John 4:7-11*
- The commandment to love. *Matthew 22:36-39*

Everyday Life Application

Love is often defined as a feeling. Take a moment to look at the different definitions of love. What definition of love comes closest to how charity is used in *I Corinthians 13*?

Author: Minister Sophia Eaves

Lesson 18 January 28, 2023
Shevat 6, 5783

THEY DESIRE A BETTER COUNTRY

Introduction

Faith is one of the most important concepts in the Bible. Based on the simple definition of belief in *Hebrews 11:1;* faith is sometimes misunderstood. It is frequently oversimplified as an oral profession or misapplied to works alone. Faith originates in the realm of the unseen. According to the Scriptures, we walk by faith and not by sight. Faith is an individual persuasion that must not only be in the mouth of the believer, but also in the heart. True faith emanating from the heart will be demonstrated in action that are often times unexplainable to the natural man.

Memory Verse *Hebrews 11:16* But now they desire a better country, that is, an heavenly: wherefore God is not ashamed to be called their God: for he hath prepared for them a city.

Biblical Application

Hebrews 11 begins by defining faith and providing individual demonstrations of faith by Abel, Enoch, Noah, Abraham, and Sara. The faith of each person was evident in their actions. Sacrifices were made that cost them something. From the gift of firstlings and fat by Abel to the righteous living of Enoch. Noah acted from a place of reverence for God. He took heed to instructions from God about things that had not been seen. It took tremendous faith for Abraham to leave his home and the majority of his family go to a place that remained to be seen. Although Sara initially laughed at the promise of God, she later judged God faithful through faith. These all made life changing decisions because of something they had never seen. They also died in faith not having received the promises. None of them were mindful of what they had forsaken. There were no regrets. Their primary focus was obtaining a better country not of this world and its goods. May our focus be so directed towards obtaining a heavenly country and eternal life with Christ that we are willing to forsake all in faith.

- Sacrifice to make it to a better country. *Hebrews 11:1-16.*
- Take up your cross and follow Jesus. *Matthew 16: 24-27.*
- Our hope is not in this life. *II Corinthians 5: 1-10; I Corinthians 15: 19.*

Everyday Life Application

How has your faith required sacrifice? Reflect on ways you walked in faith acting on God's Word and not walking by sight.

Lesson 19 February 4, 2023
Shevat 13, 5783

THE POWER OF PRAYER

Introduction

As we walked toward the altar, the singer said, don't forget the family prayer, Jesus is going to meet you there, when you gather around at the altar, don't forget the family prayer. Prayer will travel across the ocean, prayer will travel across the sea, prayer will make you love one another, and prayer will keep your home in peace. This song shares a truth that prayer can go to places where we cannot go, can reach to places we cannot reach. Sometimes our prayers can be long but other times it can simply be, help me Jesus. God has given us such a powerful tool to develop and cultivate a meaningful relationship with him and that is prayer. The enemy recognizes the power of prayer. Many times, he distracts us with a variety of methods such as social media, tv, and the busyness of life to hinder us from developing a consistent and effective prayer life. As we go through this lesson, consider the examples in the scripture of the power and impact of prayer.

Memory Verse *James 5:16* Confess your faults one to another, and pray one for another, that ye may be healed. The effectual fervent prayer of a righteous man availeth much.

Biblical Application

In his book, Magnificent Prayer, Nick Harrison states prayer is truly, wonderfully, amazingly magnificent. Prayer is an invitation to us from God Himself, asking us to please communicate with Him. Through prayer we speak to Almighty God and Almighty God speaks to us. Through prayer we ask for and receive good things from our heavenly Father. We, in our humanity, too often lose the sense of just how marvelous, how tremendous, how magnificent, and powerful prayer really can be. Rather than burdensome and often passive Christian duty, prayer should be an active Christian pleasure for every believer.

Isn't it amazing that Jesus took the time to pray? Think about that for a moment. Jesus the son of God who thought it not robbery to be equal with God took time to pray. This alone should make us realize how important prayer is to the believer. Jesus modeled for his disciples the example of consistently praying.

- Jesus gave us an example of prayer. *Matthew 14:22-23; Luke 6:12-16; Mark 1:29-37.*
- During one of his most challenging moments, Jesus prayed. *Matthew 26:36-46.*
- Jesus's prayer life impacted his disciples and caused them to ask Jesus to teach them how to pray. *Luke 11:1-4.*
- Take comfort, Jesus has prayed for us. *John 17:20-26.*

Everyday Life Application

Prayer is our time to spend with and communicate with God. What are ways you have developed a consistent and fruitful prayer life? Share this with others in the class.

Take action: The You Version Bible app is a great way to engage with the Bible every day. Check out the section that prompts you to go through a daily guided prayer. I am sure you will enjoy.

Author: Deacon Walter H. Preston, Jr.

Lesson 20 February 11, 2023
Shevat 20, 5783

A TOUCH

Introduction

Before reaching the town of Gennesaret, Jesus had performed at least 20 miracles, and his fame was growing. When he reached Gennesaret, the men of the city recognized Jesus, they sent word that Jesus was in town. A crowd of people soon formed, and those who were sick or had diseases pushed to touch Jesus' garment believing they would be made whole.

Memory Verse *Matthew 14:36* And besought him that they might only touch the hem of his garment: and as many as touched were made perfectly whole.

Biblical Application

God has the power and authority to heal. In the scriptures he said, "I wound, and I heal. . ." He decides who will be healed, as he has mercy on whom he wishes. God used his servants to heal. Moses interceded for Miriam to be healed, Abraham interceded for Abimelech and his household to be healed, and there were others. In the New Testament, Jesus and his disciples performed many healing miracles. Jesus healed people who were blind, paralyzed, had hand atrophy, and hearing or speech impairments. Faith in Jesus was paramount to being made whole. Even family members and friends had faith that Jesus could heal their loved one or friend. When modern medicine fails to successfully treat or cure sickness and disease, we can still access the power of healing through the Holy Ghost. We cannot touch Jesus' garment, but we can call upon the ministry to pray the prayer of faith, anoint with oil and lay hands on the sick. Today, we will learn more about healing that is available through physicians, medicine and the prayer of faith.

- God has the authority and power to heal if it is his will. *Exodus 15:26, 23:25; Deuteronomy 32:39; Psalm 103:1-3; Romans 9:18.*
- God allows medicine to provide relief and healing. *2 Kings 20:7; Isaiah 1:6, 38:21; Jeremiah 8:22, 51:8.*
- Physicians can treat sickness and disease, but God is ultimately the healer. *Matthew 9:12; Colossians 4:14.*
- The ministry has healing power through the Holy Ghost. *Matthew 10:1; James 5:14-16.*
- Faith and obedience are essential for healing. *II Kings 5:1-14; Matthew 9:27-31; Mark 2:3-5, 10-12, 5:25-34, 10:46-52; Luke 17:11-19.*

Everyday Life Application

Eating a proper diet, getting an annual physical exam, exercising regularly, and taking prescribed medications, if needed, can support better health and health outcomes. What part, if any, do you play in supporting healing in your body?

Author: Minister Sophia Eaves

Lesson 21 February 18, 2023
Shevat 27, 2023

THINGS WHICH CANNOT BE SHAKEN

Introduction

Israel was captive for 70 years in Babylon. Following the captivity, God spoke to them through the prophet Haggai. The people were so concerned with their own houses and life they were not about their Father's business. In chapter one, The Lord admonished them to consider their ways. They were sowing but not harvesting; eating, drinking, and clothed but not satisfied. They even had jobs and earned wages but couldn't save or get ahead. The Lord then brought a drought upon the land the crops, cattle and labor of men's hands. Finally, the leaders and people obeyed and began to build the temple.

Memory Verse *Hebrews 12:27* And this word, Yet once more, signifieth the removing of those things that are shaken, as of things that are made, that those things which cannot be shaken may remain.

Biblical Application

Chapter 2 contains an exhortation from the Lord to the governor, the priest, and the people. Their work seemed small and insignificant compared to the previous temple. The Lord encouraged them to be strong and work and assured them that he was with them. He told them not to fear, that his spirit remained among them. Haggai prophesied of a future time in which the Lord would shake the heavens, earth, sea, dry land and all nations. This passage is quoted in *Hebrews 12* and interpreted to signify a removal of the things that are created that those things which are eternal may remain. When are exhorted to have grace and to serve God with reverence and godly fear because we are receiving a kingdom that cannot be moved. Let us remain focused on the spiritual and the eternal work that God has assigned us. Avoid being discouraged by comparing your ministry to others or to a former time in the church. As long as we are working towards spreading the gospel of Jesus Christ, we can rest assured the Lord is with us.

- Consider your ways. *Haggai 1:1-14.*
- Be strong and do the will of God. *Haggai 2: 1-9.*
- Focus on the things that cannot be shaken. *Hebrews 12:18-29.*

Everyday Life Application

Do a personal assessment of your contribution to the body of Christ. How can you become involved in the work of the kingdom of God?

Lesson 22 February 25, 2023
Adar 4, 5783

GOD IS WORKING

Introduction

Merriam-Webster defines *create* as to bring into existence, to produce or bring about by a course of action or behavior, to produce through imaginative skill. Creation equals action, and action equals movement, and movement equals work. There is immense power in being productive. Ideas become tangible items through the application of energy. Through computer-aided design (CAD), a blank screen becomes an architectural drawing. Architectural drawings are transformed into homes by assembling building materials according to schematics. Buildings are constructed, books are written, programs are developed and initiated, and so on and so forth, through action, which is force applied over time (Stehle, 1993)[5]. The US Labor Day holiday was instituted to celebrate the many achievements of the nation's workers (U.S. Department of Labor, 2022). But long before this holiday, we see the institution of work celebrated in the mighty works of the creation. For a preeminent example of the power of work, look no further than God, the Creator, who has been working since day one.

Memory Verse *John 5:17* But Jesus answered them, My Father worketh hitherto, and I work.

Biblical Application

---

[5] (Stehle, 1993) Stehle, Philip M. (1993). "Least-action principle". In Parker, S. P. (ed.). *McGraw-Hill Encyclopedia of Physics* (2nd ed.). New York: McGraw-Hill. p. 670. ISBN 0-07-051400-3. "History of Labor Day" U.S. Department of Labor, https://www.dol.gov/general/laborday/history (accessed April 2, 2022)

Our first introduction to God in the scriptures lets us know that from the very beginning, He was making things happen. *Genesis 1:1* states, "In the beginning God created the heaven and the earth." When persecuted for healing a man on the Sabbath, Jesus' rebuttal shed light on God's attributes of being a worker. We do not serve an idle God. The term "rested" in *Genesis 2:2* does not mean that God took a nap, as *Psalm 121:4* tells us God never sleeps or slumbers. Rather, "rested" in Genesis the second chapter, according to Strong's Concordance, refers to God's completion of the creation work. Rest assured, He never stopped being effective in the Heavens or the Earth. Even when we can't see it, He's still being productive. And what's more, the fruits of His labor are flawless and wonderful. We can be comforted in the knowledge that we serve a working God. He is our shining example to work. *Exodus 20:10* instructs us to rest from our labors on the seventh day, but before this, verse 9 says, "Six days shalt thou labour, and do all thy work."

- From the beginning, God is working: *Genesis 1:1; John 5:17; Philippians 2:13; Psalm 74:12.*
- Even when we can't see it with the natural eye, God is working: *Genesis 1:3-4, 13-18; 2 Kings 6:8-17.*
- The fruits of God's labor are good! *Genesis 1:4, 10, 12, 18, 21, 25, 31; Romans 8:28; Philippians 1:6.*
- Just as God is working, we should be working: *John 6:28-29; Ephesians 2:10; 1 Corinthians 3:9; John 9:4.*

Everyday Life Application

A seed is sown in the soil, positioned in the light, and provided water; however, a plant doesn't grow out of the ground overnight. But if you keep watering that seed, with light and nutrients, that plant *will* grow. And you will soon see the evidence of your work. Seedtime and harvest, while agricultural, can be used in many areas as an example of putting in the work to accomplish a goal. Be encouraged to keep working, as our Father in Heaven is working. You *will* see the fruits of your labor.

Author: *Deacon James Fant, Jr.*

Lesson 23 March 4, 2023
Adar 11, 5783

THOU GOOD AND FAITHFUL SERVANT

Introduction

The Lord instructs us to behold, the heavens and the earth with all that is therein belong to him (*Deuteronomy10:14)*. The earth is the Lords and the fulness thereof; the world, and they that dwell therein *(Psalm 24:1)*. Every beast of the forest is his, and the cattle on a thousand hills. He knows every fowl of the mountains and the wild beasts of the field are his (*Psalm 50:10-11*). The Lord is the creator and owner of all things. As his servants he has entrusted certain things to us in stewardship. How we utilize the resources he has allocated to us is a factor in where we spend eternity.

Memory Verse *Matthew 25:21* His lord said unto him, Well done, thou good and faithful servant: thou hast been faithful over a few things, I will make thee ruler over many things: enter thou into the joy of thy lord.

Biblical Application

The parable of the talents provides guidance for us as stewards of the Lord's goods here on earth. The word "talent" is used in *Matthew 25* and "pound" is used in *Luke 19*. Both terms commonly refer a sum of money (Strong's & New Unger's Dictionary)[6]. In *Luke 19:13*, the nobleman instructs his servants to occupy (busy oneself or trade) until he comes (Strong's Dictionary). The Lord has entrusted each of us with a varying amount of his money while here on earth. Let us be careful how we trade or occupy his money. The servant who hid his money and did nothing with it was called

---

[6] The New Unger's Bible Dictionary. Merrill F. Unger 1988. Moody Bible Institute of Chicago.

wicked, slothful, and an enemy. *Luke 19:14, 27* reveals this was a rejection of the noblemen (Jesus) and his authority. At the minimum, using his financial resources wisely involves at gaining interest in a stable investment. We must be found faithful over that which is given to us in order to become ruler over more. Sometimes, our financial losses result from a lack of diligence with that which is given to us. Utilization of resources such as financial advisors and education in finance are part of being wise stewards of the Lord's goods.

- What type of servant are you? *Luke 19:11-27; Matthew 25:14-30.*
- Proper money management is important. *Ecclesiastes 10:19; I Timothy 6: 6-10.*
- The Lord owns everything. *Deuteronomy 10:14; Psalm 24:1, 50:10-12.*

Everyday Life Application

Take time to assess your stewardship. Have you improved your money management skills over time?

Lesson 24 March 11, 2021
Adar 18, 5783

YE SHALL NOT TEMPT THE LORD YOUR GOD

Introduction

Satan tempted Jesus by setting him on a pinnacle of the temple and trying to get him to throw himself off. The adversary tried to get him to act in pride to prove he was the Son of God. God allowed Jesus to be tested by Satan and allows his servants to have their faith tested. Our response to testing demonstrates if we truly trust and believe God. To make unwise decisions and expect God's miraculous intervention is to fall for the trick of the adversary and tempt the Lord.

Memory Verse *Deuteronomy 6:16* Ye shall not tempt the LORD your God, as ye tempted him in Massah.

Biblical Application

The children of Israel saw the plagues upon the Egyptians, were led by a pillar of cloud and fire through the wilderness of the Red Sea. However, they demonstrated fear and a lack of trust in the Lord before crossing Red Sea. Then after crossing the Red Sea, they consistently murmured(complained) against Moses when they didn't have water or food. In Rephidim, they chided(quarreled) with Moses about the lack of water to the point where they were ready to stone him (Strong's Dictionary). They questioned whether the Lord was among them or not. The Lord allowed them to cross the Red Sea on dry land, fed them with manna and quail, provided good water, but the people still did not trust Him. Instead of dwelling in Him and believing the Lord would provide they doubted whether God was even with them. Those who have true faith in Christ, believe his Word and demonstrate this through daily trust and obedience. They do not need to jump off buildings, handle poisonous snakes, or deliberately drink poison to prove God is real and his Word his true.

We may get thirsty; our faith may get tested in the difficulties of this life; but Jesus gave us an assurance that he is with us always, even unto the end of the world.

- A lack of trust in action. *Exodus 14:11-12, 15:24, 16:2-4.*
- Israel tempts the Lord. *Exodus 17:1-7.*
- The Lord allows saints to be tested. *Matthew 4:1-11; Psalm 17:1-3, 66:10-12; Job 23:1-12.*

Everyday Life Application

When Jesus was tested by Satan, he quoted God's Word. Let us prayerfully read, memorize, and meditate upon the Word daily to endure testing

Lesson 25 March 18, 2023
Adar 25, 5783

AVENGE NOT YOURSELVES

Introduction

Romans 12:1-2 are frequently quoted verses. However; details on how to accomplish our reasonable service and to not be conformed to this world are often omitted. What is involved in being transformed by the renewing of your mind? Paul goes on to include many exhortations for holy living in *Romans 12*. Practicing love is a prevalent theme. The love of Christ goes beyond just loving those who love us. True love involves not avenging ourselves; but blessing our enemies. Sometimes we encounter evil in this life perpetrated by those we encounter at work, school, church, and amongst family. How you respond to enemies is a measure your transformation or your conformation to this world.

Memory Verse *Romans 12:19* Dearly beloved, avenge not yourselves, but rather give place unto wrath: for it is written, Vengeance is mine; I will repay, saith the Lord.

Biblical Application

II Timothy 4:14 provides an example of Paul's reaction to evil he encountered in this life. The Bible does not provide explicit details as to what was done to Paul. Alexander the coppersmith did him much evil and greatly withstood the gospel. Paul warned Timothy about Alexander, but left justice up to the Lord. As believers, we trust and acknowledge the sovereignty of God by not seeking personal revenge. This does not negate the concept of advocating for and pursuing Scriptural righteousness in this evil world. In *Acts 6-7* Stephen encountered evil from those of the synagogue for preaching Jesus Christ. He was brought before the council and high priest, then was stoned to death for proclaiming the gospel. The final words of Stephen before his death were a prayer that those who stoned him would be forgiven. Jesus Christ provided the greatest example of how to love enemies and bless those who persecute us. When persecuted by the religious crowd, he was forsaken by his disciples. Jesus then died for sins that he never committed rather than seeking revenge. Remember that while we were yet sinners Christ died for us!

- Be not conformed to this world. *Romans 12: 1-21; Deuteronomy 32:35-36 I Thessalonians 5:14-18.*
- Love your enemies. *Acts 7:54-60; Matthew 5:38-48.*

Everyday Life Application

Do you pray for your enemies and bless those that persecute you? If you seek revenge on someone, who did you wrong, does it exhibit a lack of trust in the Lord?

Lesson 26 March 25, 2023
Abib 3, 5783

SIN

Introduction

Sin entered the human race with Adam's transgression. According to Scripture, sin is universal *(Romans 5:12*). All are born under. Adam represented all of the created order since he was given dominion over it by God. Sin and death came by Adam, righteousness and life by Jesus Christ.

Memory Verse Romans *3:5-6* But if our unrighteousness commend the righteousness of God, what shall we say? Is God unrighteous who taketh vengeance? (I speak as a man) God forbid: for then how shall God judge the world?

Biblical Application

God is holy. God abhors (regard with disgust and hatred) sin. God does not treat sin lightly. In Scripture, God prescribes the death penalty for sin (*Rom. 6:23*). The biblical definition of sin is defined in Scripture as, the Transgression of the Law. All unrighteousness is sin *(I John 3:4; 5:17*). Sin is judged by God.

- The characteristics of sin. *Deuteronomy 9:7; Proverbs 24:9; Isaiah 1:18; Hebrews 3:13; James 1:15, 4:17.*
- Sin is repulsive (arousing intense distaste or disgust) to God. *Genesis 6:5-6; II Samuel 11:27; Psalm 5: 4, -5; 106:40; Proverbs 15: 8-9; Luke 16:15.*
- Sin is repulsive to the righteous. *Psalm 26: 5, 9; Proverbs 8:13; Romans 7:15, 19, 23-24; Revelation 2:2.*
- Sin must be repented of and confessed. *Psalm 38:18; Proverbs 28:13; I John 1:9.*

Sin excludes (to deny someone access to or bar someone from a place, group, or privilege) from the kingdom of God. *I Corinthians 6: 9, 10; Ephesians 5:5; Revelation. 21:27.*

- Sin is known to God. *Job 10:14; 11:11; 14:16, 17; 34: 21, 22; Psalm 69:5; Jeremiah 2:22.*
- Sin separates from Him. *Isaiah 59:1-2, 64:7; Micah 3:4; Luke 13:27.*

Everyday Life Application

Confess personal sins and profess faith in Christ. Jesus is the one who intercedes before God on behalf of the sinner. My little children, these things write I unto you, that you sin not. And if any man sin, we have an advocate with the Father, Jesus Christ the righteous. And he is the propitiation for our sins: and not for ours only, but also for the sins of the whole world.

Author: Evangelist Irene Crawford

Lesson 27 April 1, 2023
Abib 10, 5783

GOD'S PASSION FOR CHRIST

Introduction

I see God through the lens of his Word. His word gives a glimpse of the love he has for humanity. I can see God the master architect, as he looked at creating us. God determine we would be made in his imagine and in his likeness. He did not create us just any abstract shape or being. God fearfully and wonderfully made us. Having the knowledge that we are made in his image and likeness speaks volumes. He made us with a mind to reason and emotions to feel. He put in man complex systems like the nervous system, a digestive system, reproductive system etc. But he also knew we were but flesh. God understood we would fall and be alienated from him, a Holy God. For this reason, he already had a plan for our redemption in the person of Christ Jesus!

Memory Verse *Isaiah 53:10* Yet it pleased the LORD to bruise him; he hath put him to grief: when thou shalt make his soul an offering for sin, he shall see his seed, he shall prolong his days, and the pleasure of the LORD shall prosper in his hand.

Biblical Application

God understood the full scoop of humanities, unholy nature, The injustices we would inflict on each other, the things our evil imagination would conjure up and the inhuman act we would commit to each other. God determined that the wages of our sin would be death. For these reasons, there was a passion for the manifestation of Jesus Christ. God's love for us was the driving force to become *visible, touchable, to be wrapped in* sinful flesh. In addition, to be tempted in all points like we are; to shed his own blood and then lay down his own life; just so we could live and not die. This is an awesome picture of God's passion for Christ!

- His Passion. *John 3: 14-18.*
- Just for us. *Isaiah 53: 1-12*
- Then end goal. *Colossians 1: 1-23.*

Everyday Life Application

What other scriptures can you rehearse to remind you of God's intense love for us?

Author: Evangelist Patricia Powell

Lesson F5 April 6, 2023
Abib 15, 5783

PASSOVER AND FEAST OF UNLEAVENED BREAD

Introduction

Scripture declares Jesus Christ to be the lamb without blemish or spot foreordained and slain before the foundation of the world *(I Peter 1:19-20, Revelation 13:8)*. At the appointed time, thousands of years after creation; Jesus Christ became our Passover. The Lord's plan of redemption for humanity was perfectly executed. Multiple prophecies were fulfilled by the sovereign power of God. Numerous people from various walks of life were used to fulfill God's plan in their own ignorance. Even Satan himself was used by God to bring about the redemption of mankind at the Lord's feast.

Memory Verse *John 12:27* Now is my soul troubled; and what shall I say? Father, save me from this hour: but for this cause came I unto this hour.

Biblical Application

The hidden wisdom of God was ordained before the world unto our glory. None of the princes of this world knew: for had they known it, they would not have crucified the Lord of glory *(I Corinthians 2:7-8)*. *Acts 13:27* declares, for they that dwell at Jerusalem, and their rulers, because they knew him not, nor yet the voices of the prophets which are read every sabbath day, they have fulfilled them in condemning him. The chief priests, scribes, and elders were not focused on observing Passover, but sought occasion on how take Jesus subtilty and to kill him. Satan entered Judas and influenced him to covenant with them to betray Jesus for money. Jesus spoke openly to his disciples about his betrayal and crucifixion. Yet the reality of what was about to come to pass was hidden from them. As he rode into Jerusalem on the colt of an ass and the people took palm branches out to meet him; the disciples did not understand what was taking place. Neither did they realize God placed it in the heart of the woman with the alabaster box to anoint him for his burial. *Psalm 22* was fulfilled in great detail at the crucifixion of Jesus. We are blessed to have the revelation of the Scriptures and the Holy Ghost as we observe the feast.

- We are blessed to understand. *John 12:1-41 Psalm 22: 1-18.*
- Used by God. *Luke 22:1-13.*
- Jesus died for you. *Isaiah 53:1-12.*

Everyday Life Application

Reflect on the blessings you have enjoyed since you began observance of the Lord's Passover. How can we share with others the blessings involved in feast observance?

Lesson 28 April 8, 2023
Abib 17, 5783

GROOMING OUR SUCCESSORS

Introduction

From the onset of scripture, it's easy to recognize that God is a God of purpose. God in his foreknowledge, lay's out a master plan with a specific goal and agenda. There are no haphazard moves with him. With his purposes in mind, He can and often uses people to accomplish what He wills. There is a unique challenge with God using mankind, and the challenge is that He deals in large blocks of time. *James 4:14* points to the fact that man's life is like a vapor that appears for a little while then vanishes away. God's purpose may start with one man and conclude with someone else. In truth we only have a short window of opportunity. With this reality in mind, it is vitally important to work for the kingdom and groom the next generation to take the reins of leadership in whatever capacity God sees fit.

Memory Verse *Proverbs 22:6* Train up a child in the way he should go and when he is old, he will not depart from it.

Biblical Application

Grooming our successors involves teaching, correcting, giving wisdom, and modifying behavior to be Christ like. Providing these tools allows our successors to walk in a spirit of excellence, in the capacity or role a person is meant to occupy. Many of the lessons learned will not only be by verbal communication, but also by observations; for this reason, it is important the mentor (spiritual, father, leader) be Christ like and walk in the spirit of excellence. The objective is to have the body of Christ and the works of God, operate like a well-oiled machine. When one completes their role or goes on to be with the Lord, there should be no lack in knowledge and understanding in continuing the works that has been left vacant. The works of God are not done, and if the Lord should continue to tarry, this generation may possibly be succeeded by other generations.

Passing the mantle.

- Moses & Joshua. *Exodus 24:13; Exodus 17:9-10; Numbers 27:18-23.*
- Elijah & Elisha. *I Kings 19:16-19; II Kings 2: 1-14.*
- David & Solomon. *I Chronicles 22: 1-9, 17-19; I Chronicles 28: 1-10.*
- Jesus & the disciples. *John 13:5-13; John 17: 6-17; Acts 1: 3-9.*
- Paul & Timothy. *Acts 16: 1-4; I Timothy 1: 1-4; II Timothy 4: 1-5.*

Everyday Life Application

Are there some common threads that run through these 5 bullet points? If so, what are some of them? Discuss how to implement, if possible, mentoring programs.

Author: *Elder James Taylor, Jr.*

Lesson F6 April 12, 2023
Abib 21, 5783

THE FEAST OF UNLEAVENED BREAD

Introduction

In *I Corinthians 11*, Paul set in order some issues concerning the observance of this feast. There were issues with divisions, lack of focus, and a lack of sincerity. The primary purpose for the observance was supposed to be remembrance of Jesus. However, many church members made it more about themselves than Christ. Some were drunken, others came for food, and others ate out of order. The approach to taking communion today in the body of Christ is similar in some ways to that which occurred at Corinth.

Memory Verse *I Corinthians 11:26* For as often as ye eat this bread, and drink this cup, ye do shew the Lord's death till he come.

Biblical Application

The phrase "as often as" ye eat or drink is misinterpreted to mean communion can be taken whenever believers want to. This Greek word cluster is only used one other place, in *Revelation 11:6.* There the phrase is "as often as they will", the addition of the words" they will" indicates the two witnesses had a choice to do as they desired or willed. This feast was commanded by the Lord to be kept once a year for the specific purpose of showing the Lord's death and in remembrance of Jesus Christ. Another issue at Corinth, was eating and drinking unworthily (irreverently) (Strong's Dictionary). This lack of reverence resulted in severe consequences for some. As we keep this glorious feast, let us examine ourselves and keep it with the utmost reverence for Jesus Christ. In remembrance of him means so much to each of us. Think about all that Jesus Christ delivered you from. As an innocent man, he suffered the humiliation of being mocked, spit upon, had his beard pulled out, was scourged, crucified, and died because he loved us! What a privilege and honor we have to celebrate this feast and show his death to others.

- Remember Jesus with reverence. *I Corinthians 11:17-33; Luke 22:15-19; Leviticus 23: 2-8.*
- Such were some of you. *I Corinthians 6:9-11.*
- Let all things be done decently and in order. *I Corinthians 14:26-40.*

Everyday Life Application

Reflect on your own worship and feast observance. How can you be more reverent and Christ focused?

Lesson 29 April 15, 2023
Abib 24, 5783

CONSIDER THE RAVENS

Introduction

Excessive worrying has no positive effects. In fact, scientific literature tells us that prolonged stress can be detrimental to physical well-being (Dhabhar 2014, Bruce 2020)[7]. Short-term stress, like fight or flight, is advantageous during temporary traumatic events. But long-term stress can have deleterious effects on the heart, the brain, and even the immune system (Bruce 2020). Merriam Webster defines worry as mental distress or agitation resulting from concern usually for something impending or anticipated. People commonly worry about money, their relationships with others, and even their health, which is ironic because excessive worry is harmful for good health. At its core, excessive worry is fueled by feelings of insecurity and insufficiency. But thanks be to God! In His infinite wisdom, He has given us everything we need. So, we don't need to worry.

Memory Verse *Luke 12:24* Consider the ravens: for they neither sow nor reap; which neither have storehouse nor barn; and God feedeth them: how much more are ye better than the fowls?

---

[7] Anxieties.com:http://www.anxieties.com
Anxiety Disorders Association of America:http://www.ADAA.org
National Institute of
MentalHealth:http://www.nimh.nih.gov/healthinformation/anxietymenu.cfm
WorryWiseKids.org:http://www.worrywisekids.org
*—These resources are recommended by the authors of (Gordon 2006).
Bibliography:
Dhabhar, F.S. Effects of stress on immune function: the good, the bad, and the beautiful. Immunol Res 58, 193–210 (2014). https://doi.org/10.1007/s12026-014-8517-0
Debra Fulghum Bruce, "How Worrying Affects the Body" WebMD, September 12, 2020 https://www.webmd.com/balance/guide/how-worrying-affects-your-body

Shearer S, Gordon L. The patient with excessive worry. Am Fam Physician. 2006 Mar 15;73(6):1049-56. PMID: 16570740.

Biblical Application

In the beginning of *Luke 12,* Jesus teaches a massive crowd important lessons on the perils of hypocrisy, the power of bravery in the face of persecution, and how the Holy Spirit gives us the words to speak when in the midst of powerful people. In the middle of this awesome message, a man from the crowd interrupted and asked Jesus to take his side in a trivial financial dispute. A trivial dispute! Afterwards, Jesus warned about worrying over worldly possessions and he told the parable of the rich fool, who's problem wasn't his riches, rather, his singular focus on self-preservation. The man from the massive crowd was concerned about the wrong things. *Philippians 4:6* tells us, "Be careful for nothing; but in everything by prayer and supplication with thanksgiving let your requests be made known unto God." Strong's Concordance #3309 defines *Be careful* as to be anxious, to care for. The Greek word used in this verse (merimnaó) is the same word used in *Luke 12:22* "...take no thought." In other words, don't worry. In God we have all sufficiency and security. If God takes care of the ravens and the lilies, surely, He will take care of us!

- God provides for us. So, we don't have to worry. *Luke 12:22-31.*
- Instead of worrying, pray and be at peace. *Philippians 4:6-7.*
- Cast ALL your worries upon God because He cares for you. *1 Peter 5:6-7.*

Everyday Life Application

There is so much power in humbly realizing you need the power of God to solve your problems. Stop worrying about it. Start praying about it. Relinquish your worries and be at peace. A percentage of the population who suffer from excessive worry meet the criteria for disorders listed in the Diagnostic and Statistical Manual of Mental Disorders, 4th ed. (Gordon 2006). In addition to spiritual support, excessive worriers may require help from a medical professional.

Author: *Deacon James Fant, Jr.*

Lesson 30 April 22, 2023
Zif 1, 5783

ARE WE EXEMPT?

Introduction

Exempt is defined by Strong's Dictionary as clean, free from, clear, or innocent. In the general church world, you may have heard statements like these, "Saint don't get sick", "I don't claim that condition; God won't let me go through this" and others like it. In addition, the impression is sometimes given that if we believe enough the condition will always just go away. However, a close look at scriptures paints a very different picture. One that's based on the fact that we are all under the umbrella of a world that is contaminated by sin and the curse of death. *James 5:14* asks this question, "Is there any sick among you?" But, listening to some ministries, you could very well walk away with the impression that we as believers are exempt from the normal experiences of life.

Memory Verse. *Psalms 34:19* Many are the afflictions of the righteous: but the LORD delivereth him out of them all.~~Many are the affliction of the righteous, but the Lord delivers from them all~~

Biblical Application

Paul in *I Timothy 5:23* gives Timothy instructions for his stomach condition. Neither of these accounts is one rebuked for acknowledging an illness, as if they had no faith, but rather they were given instruction on how to deal with the conditions. The danger in promoting an unbalance look at what happens to us in real life can generate an unrealistic expectation, which can lead to disenchantment with God. Don't be mistaken, God is a promise keeper, and he keeps his word. For this reason, we cannot pick and choose what in God's word best suits us. Our days on this earth are few and are full of trouble. But we can be assured, God will never leave us nor forsake us as we progress through our journey here.

- Death promised. *Genesis 2: 17, 14-18.*
- Humanity is under the same umbrella. *Ecclesiastes 3: 1-10; I Corinthians 10:13; Job 14:1; Matthew 8:16-17.*
- God's ways for recovery. *Isaiah 38:1, 21; Luke 13: 11, 12-13; II Corinthians 12:7-8, 12:9.*
- Aligning with the will of God. *Luke 11: 1-2; Matthew 26:42; John 5:30.*

Everyday Life Application

Covid highlighted our mortality, saved or unsaved. Was your perspective changed, strengthen during that season? Share with the Class!

Author: *Evangelist Patricia Powell*

Lesson 31 April 29, 2023
Zif 8, 5783

GOD'S GLORY

Introduction

The Greek word for "glory" is doxa. This term is used to describe God's nature and actions in self-manifestation. The Three-In-One Bible Reference Companion defines "The Glory of God" as the manifestations of his nature. Scripture speak of "glory" as God's Presence. In the Old Testament, the glory of God appeared as a cloud, smoke or fire. The nation of Israel saw the glory when God came down to meet them on Mount Sinai (*Ex. 19:16*). The heavens declare God's Glory (*Psa. 19:1 - 4; 97:6)*. God made everything Beautiful *(Eccl. 3:11*). The Desert will Blossom *(Isa. 35:1, 2)*. God has revealed Himself in the beauty and order of His created world, thereby removing any excuse for ignorance of Himself *(Ro. 1:20)*. He is the "King of Glory" (*Psa. 24: 7-10)* He is the "God of Glory" *(Psa. 29:3; Acts 7:2). He is the* 'Father of Glory" *(2 Pe. 1:17; Eph. 1:17)*

Memory Verse: *Exodus 13:21 And* the Lord went before them by day in a pillar of a cloud, to lead them the way, and by night in a pillar of fire, to give the light; to go by day and night.

Biblical Application

God's inherent glory belongs to him alone. The New Testament carries over the theme of glory from the Old. But now, it is clearly applied to the Lord Jesus and the Holy Ghost. Glory is a characteristic of God seen in both the Old and New Testament descriptions of God and his presence. The word "glory" in the Bible is often used to describe the splendor, holiness and majesty of God. The Book of John connects Gods presence in giving the Law and the indwelling of the presence of God in the Tabernacle to Jesus dwelling with humanity by calling Jesus the Word.

GLORY OF GOD—*manifestations of his nature*

Manifested to:

Moses (*Exodus* 24:9-17)
Stephen (*Acts 7:55)*

Reflected in:

Christ (*John 1:14)*
Man *(1 Corinthians 11:7)*

Appearances of:

The Tabernacle (*Exodus 40: 34-38*)
The Temple (*1 Kings 8: 10, 11*)
At Jesus Birth (*Luke 2: 8-11*)

The believer's relation to:

Does all for *(1 Corinthians 10:31)*
Illuminated by *(2 Corinthians 4:6)*
Will stand in presence of (*Jude 24*)

Man's relation to:

Corrupts *(Romans 1:23)*
Falls short of *(Romans 3:23)*
Refuse to give to God *(Acts 12:23)*

Everyday Life Application

Read and study Paul's statement regarding the Glory of God in the face of Jesus Christ. (II *Corinthians 4: 3-6).*

Author: *Evangelist Irene Crawford*

Lesson 32 May 6, 2023
Zif 15, 5783

YOUR SAVIOR NEEDS YOU!

Introduction

As Jesus sat near Jacob's well, he met the woman of Samaria. He asked her to draw him water. At the time, the Jews and Samaritans did not associate with each other. While speaking with Jesus, Jesus shared with her that he was the Christ. The woman left her waterpot and went into the city and invited others to come see Jesus. She said, "Come, see a man, which told me all things that I ever did: is not this the Christ?" The woman of Samaria is an example of a witness. She had a personal experience with Jesus, and she invited others to come meet him. The Bible says those she invited "came unto him." Today, witnesses like the woman of Samaria are still needed to testify or share about Jesus Christ. People need to hear how they can be saved, healed, and delivered. Someone needs to hear your testimony. Will you be a witness?

Memory Verse: *Acts 1:8* But ye shall receive power, after that the Holy Ghost is come upon you: and ye shall be witnesses unto me both in Jerusalem, and in all Judaea, and in Samaria, and unto the uttermost part of the earth.

Biblical Application

In *Acts 1:8*, Jesus encouraged the disciples to wait for the promise of the Holy Spirit, after which they would have power and be witnesses of him in all of Judea, and in Samaria and the uttermost part of the earth. After Jesus ascended to heaven, the apostles and other followers of Christ boldly witnessed of Jesus Christ in Judea, Samaria, Cilicia, Asia, Macedonia, Italia and other countries. They were hated, jailed and killed for testifying of Jesus Christ, but they remained faithful witnesses. Because of their good works, many people believed on Jesus, were baptized, and received the Holy Spirit.

As a Christian, your personal testimony is an effective way to share your faith in Jesus Christ and encourage others to know Him. It is a sincere way to share about hope and salvation that can be found in Christ. Witnessing doesn't have to be difficult. It can be as easy as sharing how attending church services and hearing God's word helped you, and you can extend an invitation to your church. Today's lesson will provide a basic outline for witnessing and encourage you and your class to identify additional steps to help you witness about Jesus Christ.

- Pray in advance for opportunities to witness. *Colossians 4:2-3.*
- Use discretion. *Matthew 7:6; Luke 9:5; Colossians 4:5-6.*
- Start with a casual conversation. *John 4:5-30.*
- Testify about your personal experience. *Acts 2:14-15, 22-24, 29-41; 4:18-20.*
- Continue to be a faithful witness. *Acts 5:38-42; II Timothy 1:8; Titus 3:8.*

Everyday Life Application

If you are nervous, shy or fearful about sharing your personal experience with Jesus Christ, you can still be a witness. You can use tracts or religious leaflets to introduce people to Jesus Christ. Social media is a growing platform to share a personal experience. Writing is another creative way to share your testimony. What training, if any, would help you be a better witness?

Author: Minister Sophia Eaves

Lesson 33, May 13, 2023
Zif 22 5783

BUY THE TRUTH

Introduction

Today truth is often defined as relative or personal. Many believe that truth is what an individual desires it to be. Some world leaders have attempted to call falsehoods truth for personal benefit. Biblical principles rea often overlooked or only acknowledged in part based on convenience by those who claim to believe the Bible. Theologians, professors and teachers have attempted to discredit the Bible as antiquated, or untrustworthy. This lesson will examine truth as absolute and objectively defined by the Word of God.

Memory Verse Prov 23:23 Buy the truth and sell it not, also wisdom, and instruction, and understanding.

Biblical Application

At the judgment hall before Pilate, Jesus declared that He had come into the world to bear witness to the truth. Everyone that is of the truth heareth the voice of Jesus. Jesus bore witness to the truth of God's written word. Many things written hundreds of years prior in Law of Moses, the prophets, and the Psalms concerning Christ were fulfilled. Pilate asked Jesus a question that many are asking today, what is truth? The most common Hebrew word for truth in the Bible is emeth 571. It is defined as stability; certainty (Strong's Dictionary). God is not a man, that He should lie, neither the Son of Man that He should repent; hath he said and shall he not do it. Or hath he spoken and shall not make it good? Numbers 23:19. God can swear by no greater than himself. It is certain that God will bring His word to pass. In His prayer in John 17, Jesus declared the Word of God is truth and can sanctify us. With certainty and stability, we can trust the word. Let us buy the truth and sell it not, in order to buy something. One must give another an item of value such as money and/or time. This involves study, prayer meditation and labor in the word. Many are ever learning and never able to come into the knowledge of the truth. Others resist the truth and are reprobate concerning the truth. As God reveals His word to us, we must be careful not to sell it for cunningly devised fables, false science, rational or intellectual humanism.

- **Scripture is absolute truth.** John 17:17. Col 1:5-6/ II Tim 3:13-17; Daniel 10:21; Isaiah 25:1; Prov 22:20-21.
- **Be wise.** Romans 16:17-20; Jeremiah 10:1-15
- **Grace and truth came through Jesus Christ**. John 1:14-18; 14:5-11; 18:33-40.

Everyday Life Application

What do you need to do to make yourself a better workman in the word of truth?

Devise a personal plan that is practical to buy the truth or grow in God's Word.

Lesson 34 May 20, 2023
Zif 29, 5783

SECURITY OF THE SAINTS

Introduction

The Greek word for "saint" is hagios, whose basic meaning is "to set apart, " "sanctify, " or "make holy." It is almost always used in the plural, "saints." Security is freedom from, or resilience against potential harm caused by others. Beneficiaries of security may be of persons and social groups, objects and institutions, ecosystems or any other entity or phenomenon vulnerable to unwanted change. A home security system consists of different components, including motion sensors, indoor and outdoor cameras, glass break detectors, door and window sensors, yard signs and window stickers, smoke detectors, and carbon monoxide detectors. These alarm system components work together to keep you and your family safe from a variety of threats.

Memory Verse I *Peter 2:6* Wherefore also it is contained in the scripture, Behold, I lay in Sion a chief corner stone, elect, precious: and he that believeth on him shall not be confounded.

Biblical Application

In Scripture, safety of the "righteous" is assured. Safety is of the Lord. We have security in the perfect sacrifice of Jesus. God Himself is the source and He provides safety and security for the saints. In the Bible, God is a "Divine Keeper"; a "Divine Refuge". God is a "Shield". God is a "Fortress". Scripturally, everyone who has received Jesus Christ by faith is a saint. According to scripture, saints are firmly established. Saints cannot be moved. Saints are immovable. Saints are planted (*Psalm 16: 7 -9, 62:6*). As a spiritual foundation, Jesus Christ, furnishes perfect security to the saints. Security and Safety is promised to the saints. The Saints position in Christ is secure (*John 6:47; 1 John 5:12*).

Saints, or Believers are:

- Chosen and sealed by God. *Ephesians 1:3 – 23.*
- Saved by grace. Ephesians 2:1 – 10.
- United in one body. *Ephesians 2: 11- 22.*
- Equal in the body (the Mystery). *Ephesians 3: 1-21.*

Everyday Application

As, apostles, prophets, evangelists, pastors and teachers, use the gifts that He gave to equip, or provide, adjust and make ready others for service and maturity. Edify the church. Build up the body of Christ. Sing unto the LORD, O ye saints of his, and give thanks at the remembrance of his holiness.

Author: Evangelist Irene Crawford

Lesson F7 May 26, 2023
Sivan 6, 5783

DAY OF PENTECOST

Introduction

God created the hearing ear with amazing intricacy and ability. The ear's sensory receptors called hair cells, convert sound vibration into electrical signals the brain can interpret[8]. Humans are capable of hearing sounds over a range 100 trillion-fold (NIH)! God has used auditory perception to reveal himself to man since the beginning. In the garden of Eden, Adam and Eve heard the voice of God in the cool(wind) of the day (Strong's Dictionary). Noah and Abraham heard the voice of God and obeyed him. The Lord communicated to Moses and the prophets primarily through hearing.

Memory Verse *Acts 2:2* And suddenly there came a sound from heaven as of a rushing mighty wind, and it filled all the house where they were sitting.

Biblical Application

Hearing as defined in the Scriptures moves beyond just the perception of sound. The Hebrew word for hear (shama) means to hearing intelligently with the implication of attention or obedience (Strong's Dictionary). Moses called all Israel, and said unto them, Hear, O Israel, the statutes and judgments which I speak in your ears this day, that ye may learn them, and keep, and do them (*Deuteronomy 5:1*). When the day of Pentecost was fully come, the Lord choose a sound from heaven to reveal himself. The sound as of a rushing mighty wind got the attention of all those present. God filled those present with the Holy Ghost and caused them to speak with other tongues. Many churches today place great emphasis on speaking in unknown tongues. The ministry of the Holy Ghost is

[8] https://www.ncbi.nlm.nih.gov/books/NBK20366/

much more than speaking in tongues. Jesus said, when he, the Spirit of truth, is come, he will guide you into all truth *(John 16:13)*. The Holy Spirit will guide us in our hearts and thoughts if we allow him. Guidance into all truth will be according to the Word of God; which is truth (*John 17:17*). We must be diligent to exercise discernment and not override or rationalize away the Lord's guidance. Examples of the need to bring our will and emotions under subjection to the Holy Spirit include the Biblical phrases: he that hath an ear let him hear and today, if you will hear his voice (*Revelation 2:29, Hebrews 3:15*). As we celebrate this feast of Pentecost, we are thankful for the Lord's communication to us through the Holy Ghost.

- Hear O Israel. *Deuteronomy 6:1-11*
- His sheep hear his voice. John 10:1-10; Hebrews 3:1-19.
- The Comforter is come. *John 16:5-12; Acts 2:1-21*.

Everyday Life Application

How did you the Lord first communicate with you in your relationship with Him? Pray for discernment to hear, learn, keep and do communication from the Lord today.

Lesson 35 June 3, 2023
Sivan 14, 5783

LET PATIENCE HAVE HER PERFECT WORK

Introduction

Exodus 32:1 says when the people saw that Moses delayed to come down from the mountain, the people assembled about Aaron and said to him, "Come, make us a god who will go before us; as for this Moses, the man who brought us up from the land of Egypt, we do not know what has become of him." This was just one of the many times the children of Israel showed impatience. For this account the Scripture states 3,000 men lost their lives.

Memory Verse *Proverbs 3: 5-6* Trust in the LORD with all thine heart; and lean not unto thine own understanding. In all thy ways acknowledge him, and he shall direct thy paths.
~~trust in him with all your heart and lean not unto your own understanding, to always acknowledge him and he will direct your path.~~

Biblical Application

When we commit our life to Christ, he does not always give us a detailed roadmap of what to expect, when to expect, or how to expect. He simply says trust in him with all your heart and lean not unto your own understanding, to always acknowledge him and he will direct your path. The truth of the matter is, we like things quick, fast and in a hurry. Having patience is not always that easy. However, the scripture instructs us to let patience have her perfect work so we can be entire, wanting nothing. Indeed, in our walk with God, when we operate in impatience, we can invite adverse outcome for ourselves and possibly others.

- Perils of impatience. *Exodus 32: 1-5, 15-28; I Samuel 13: 4-14.*

- Virtues of patience. *Luke 21: 19; Romans 5: 1-5; Ecclesiastes 7:8; James 1: 1-4; Psalm 37:7; Psalm 40:1; Isaiah 40: 28-31.*

Everyday Life Application

What strategies can you put in place to maintain patience?

Author: Evangelist Patricia Powell

Lesson 36 June 10, 2023
Sivan 21, 5783

PUT NO DIFFERENCE

Introduction

The book of Acts contains some of the history of the early church. It provides details about the gospel being spread and gives insight into church operations shortly after the resurrection of Jesus Christ. It should be noted that observance of the seventh day Sabbath and the Feasts of the Lord continued in Acts. Questions arose concerning doctrine and proper interpretation of the Scriptures. One of the proofs of the divine inspiration of the Scriptures is evident in how the Bible interprets itself. The Word is often confirmed through God's fulfillment of prophecies found in the Psalms, the Law, and the Prophets.

Memory Verse *Acts 15:9 And* put no difference between us and them, purifying their hearts by faith.

Biblical Application

In *Acts 15,* a question arose regarding the place of circumcision in the faith of new Gentile converts to Christ. Even though the new disciples had received the Holy Ghost; certain teachers and Pharisees insisted that circumcision was necessary for salvation. Peter and the other apostles make it clear that God put no difference in Jews or Gentiles in terms of salvation. The Lord purifies the heart of believers by faith. Salvation is available to all by the grace of our Lord Jesus Christ. The determination of the council of Jerusalem did not abolish the need for obedience to God's law in the life of believers. It addressed the specific dispute over circumcision. True circumcision is now that of the heart, in the spirit and not of the letter. The determination of the counsel to abstain from meats offered to idols, and from blood, and from things strangled regarded food, but did not negate the dietary law.

- God desires the residue of men and all Gentiles seek him. *Acts 15:1-21; II Peter 3:9.*
- Circumcision is inward, by the Holy Ghost. *Romans 2:17-29; Philippians 3:1-3; Galatians 6:11-16.*
- In Christ we are all one. *Galatians 3:15-29; Ephesians 2:8-19.*

Everyday Life Application

How are you helping to fulfill the desire of God to save others?

Lesson 37 June 17, 2023
Sivan 28, 5783

THE IMPACT OF GOD'S PRESENCE

Introduction

One definition of *impact* is a significant or major effect of one thing on another. The Word of God provides many examples of God's impact on His people, stories of how He empowered them through His presence. *Matthew 1:23* spoke about His name being Emmanuel, which means God with us (God present with us). From the beginning, we see His design was to be a connected God, living in the midst of his people, even dwelling inside them in the form of His precious Holy Spirit. Because the benefits of His connection are innumerous, and there is not enough room in this lesson to list all the ways His presence impacts our lives, the lesson focuses on the joy, strength, and abundance of life that accompanies God's presence.

Memory Verse *Psalm 16:11* Thou wilt shew me the path of life: in thy presence is fulness of joy; at thy right hand there are pleasures for evermore.

Biblical Application

Psalm 16 lists benefits of a life committed to God: safety, blessings, guidance, stability, joy, pleasure, a wonderful inheritance. These benefits are eternal, unencumbered by life's circumstances. God commands us to be strong and courageous, not because of our own ability, but because He is with us. In John the 15th chapter, Jesus described our relationship as branches (us) on the vine (Him). When a branch is connected to the tree, it receives benefits from the trunk. But if the branch is cut away, it falls to the ground, withers, and dies. Likewise, we wither and die outside of God's presence. Let us stay connected to the Master and find everlasting joy, strength, and life more abundantly.

- Contentment and joy in His presence. *Psalms 16:1-11.*
- Strength and courage with God. *Joshua 1:1-9.*
- Abundant and fruitful life, only through His connection, *John 10:10; John 6:63-69; John 15:1-11.*

Everyday Life Application

Discuss the ways your life has benefited by being in God's presence.

Author: *Deacon James Fant, Jr.*

Lesson 38 June 24, 2023
Tammuz 5, 5783

THE JUST GOD

Introduction

It is no secret that Satan's mission is to kill, steal and destroy. One of his strategies is to discredit Gods motives towards humanity. He desires us to view God as an unjust God. If he can drive home this message, many will never learn to trust God's motives toward us. Is that not how he started with Eve in the Garden. Satan says to Eve, God knew when they ate of the fruit their eyes would be open and they would be as Gods knowing good and evil. Satan's argument was contrary to God's word saying don't touch or eat lest ye die. In this, Satan was planting a seed of doubt to God's real motives.

Memory *Deuteronomy 32: 4* He is the Rock, his work is perfect: for all his ways are judgement: a God of truth and without iniquity, just and right is he.

Biblical Application

Throughout Scripture we can find accounts of God's judgement for a situation. Indeed, in our limited knowledge and understanding of the ways of God, may deem these judgements questionable. Even in our lifetime we encounter situations that leave us with questions. In those times we must always know, God has all authority, period. However, not only is God Sovereign, but He is also just (Lawful, righteous). We can take comfort in a God that is righteous, along with having all authority. God does not operate with unrighteous motives. He is holy and he simply ask that we be the same (*I Peter 1:16*).

- God is just in motives. *John 10: 10-11; I Timothy 2: 1-4.*
- God is just to humanity. *Matthew 5:45; John 3: 16; Mark 13:10.*
- God is just in judgement. *Ezekiel 18: 1-32.*

Everyday Life Application

Have you ever found yourself wondering why God allows the things that he does? What do you do to keep the mind set "God is a Just God"?

Author: Evangelist Patricia Powell

Lesson 39 July 1, 2023
Tammuz 12, 5783

KEEP YOUR EYES ON THE PRIZE!

Introduction

Batters must keep their eye on the ball amid the boos. Quarterbacks must keep their eyes downfield, despite defenders trying to tackle them. Free throw shooters must focus on the basketball goal, even when opposing fans wave large funny photos in their faces. These are all sports references; however, they teach us a lot about dealing with real life distractions. David Villa, a CEO, best-selling author, and orator said, "Distraction is anything preventing us from giving our full attention to a task. When you're working toward a goal ... a distraction will take you off course and make it impossible to keep your mind on your purpose..." He went on to say that he discovered that avoidance of distractions kept his mind focused on the goal (Villa, 2016)[9]. Our goal above all should be living a life that is pleasing to God. We can't let anyone, or anything take our eyes off the prize.

Memory Verse *Philippians 3:14* I press toward the mark for the prize of the high calling of God in Christ Jesus

Biblical Application

In *II Corinthians 11:23-28* the Apostle Paul lists the afflictions he faced: stripes, prison, beatings, stonings, shipwreck, waters, robbers, perils, false brethren, weariness, toil, sleeplessness, hunger and thirst, cold and nakedness. But *Philippians 3:13-14* illustrates that Paul wasn't focused on temporary problems. Instead, he had the

---

[9] *(Villa, 2016) "When Setting Goals, Use Direction To Get Rid Of Distraction" David Villa, 2016. https://www.forbes.com/sites/forbesagencycouncil/2016/10/04/when-setting-goals-use-direction-to-get-rid-of-distraction/?sh=6b8c2caa2845*

faith to focus on the eternal prize. Strong's Concordance #1377 defines *I press* as to aggressively chase, like a hunter pursuing a catch (or a prize). Used positively, it means to earnestly pursue with all haste. Every ounce of our energy must be focused on pleasing the Father, for then will we be fruitful in every good work and grow in the knowledge of God (*Colossians 1:10*).

- Peter focused on the wind and was afraid. *Matthew 14:28-31.*
- Martha was distracted by many things, but Mary focused on Jesus. *Luke 10:38-42.*
- Lay aside every weight, and sin, and instead look to Jesus. *Hebrews 12:1-3.*
- For perfect peace, keep your mind on God. *Isaiah 26:3.*

Everyday Life Application

When driving, taking your eyes off the road for even a few seconds can be disastrous. That's why we see large LED road signs that blare "Stay Alive! Don't Text and Drive!" Likewise, we must always keep our eyes on the Master. We cannot let trials and tribulations distract us from a life of peace and happiness. This is why reading the Word of God daily is so important. Whatever you're dealing with, find the scripture that applies and fight back with the Word of God. Fill your playlist with songs of praise and victory. Pray continually and look to God. He will give you peace in the time of storm. Don't get distracted!

Author: Deacon James Fant, Jr.

Lesson 40 July 8, 2023
Tammuz 19, 5783

ETERNAL DEATH

Introduction

John, one of the twelve disciples, had been exiled to the island of Patmos because he taught about Jesus. While on Patmos, God gave John a vision of the final days of earth, and a peak at heaven. In the vision, John saw the Holy City, Jerusalem, coming down from heaven to the new earth, for the old earth had been destroyed *(Revelation 21:1-7).*

Memory Verse *Revelation 21:8* But the fearful, and unbelieving, and the abominable, and murderers, and whoremongers, and sorcerers, and idolaters, and all liars, shall have their part in the lake which burneth with fire and brimstone: which is the second death.

Biblical Application

The Book of Revelation frequently describes and warns about the second death. Jesus promises the churches that believers will not be impacted by the second death (*Revelation 2:11*) In the Bible, the Apostle Paul warns of a sharp contrast between the glorious destiny of overcomers and believers at the advent of Christ, and the fate of the impenitent (unrepentant) wicked II *Thessalonians 1: 7-9).* The Apostle John describes the Future Judgement for unbelievers and those whose names were not found written in the Book of Life. In Scripture, the second death reference the lake of fire. Accordingly, the lake of fire is reserved for the devil, the beast, the false prophet, death, hell and whosoever was not found written in the book of life. This is the second death. The second death is the eternal separation of a person from God.

- The eternal duration of the sufferings of the lost. *Isaiah 66:23, 24; Matthew 25: 41-46.*
- Justice will not be spared. *Jude 6-8.*

- Fire that shall not be quenched. *Mark 9:44, 46, 48; Luke 3:17.*
- The smoke of their torment ascending up for ever and ever. *Isaiah 34:10; Revelation 14:10-11.*
- The first resurrection and the lake of fire. *Revelation 20: 1 - 15.*

Everyday Life Application

Believers in every age, reach out into all the world with the Good News of the gospel. Accept Christ, it is the only way to avoid the lake of fire. He that believeth on the Son hath everlasting life: and he that believeth not the Son shall not see life; but the wrath of God abideth on him.

Author: Evangelist Irene Crawford

Lesson 41 July 15, 2023
Tammuz 26, 5783

MOSES' DISCIPLES

Introduction

The Pharisees took great pride in calling themselves Moses' disciples. They were self-proclaimed experts in the law of God. Jesus described them as sitting in Moses' seat. In Biblical times, this type of seat referred to an exalted seat occupied by men of great rank or influence. The Pharisees considered themselves successors of Moses in explaining and defending the law (Unger). Their religious authority was derived from their expertise and historical observance of the law of Moses. One of the reasons the chief priests and Pharisees conspired to kill Jesus was because they did not want to lose their place and nation.

Memory Verse *Acts 13:39* And by him all that believe are justified from all things, from which ye could not be justified by the law of Moses.

Biblical Application

Misunderstandings concerning the relevancy and application God's law have existed for thousands of years. The Jews sought justification through works of the law. This was impossible to accomplish through the law because all have broken the law (*Romans 3:23*). *Romans 9:31-32* says, but Israel, which followed after the law of righteousness, hath not attained to the law of righteousness. Wherefore? Because they sought it not by faith, but as it were by the works of the law. For they stumbled at that stumbling stone. In *Acts 13*, Paul preached to the Jews at Antioch the forgiveness of sins and justification through belief in Jesus Christ. He quoted *Habakkuk 1:5* warning them about their unbelief concerning the work that God worked and declared to them. Their rejection of Jesus and the Word of God resulted in them judging themselves unworthy of eternal life. The conversation that Jesus had with the Jewish leader Nicodemus, reiterates the importance of faith. Jesus made it clear salvation is through belief in him and unbelief results in condemnation. Observance of the law is not made void through faith, rather it is established. As believers we rightly divide the Word of God to discern the relevancy of observing God's law.

- Justified by Jesus. *Acts 13:13-46.*
- Unbelief results in self-condemnation. *John 3:1-21.*
- Observe and do. *Matthew 23:1-12; Romans 3:21-31.*

Everyday Life Application

As a church that observes the law of God, how can we avoid being like Moses' disciples?

Lesson 42 July 22, 2023
Av 4, 5783

THE SPIRITUAL SENSES

Introduction

It has been traditionally recognized that man has 5 natural senses (seeing, hearing, touch, taste and smell). These senses are vitally important, for they help one gather information, navigate this world, and complete and fulfill everyday tasks. They are often critical to the success of man in this life. Just as there are natural senses, God can and often opens up to man, spiritual sense. These senses, in particular, sight and hearing, allow one to gather information from the spirit of God, that the natural mind and senses are oblivious too, for they are spiritually discerned. Like the natural senses, these spiritual senses give one access to information that can give comfort, open understanding, provide direction, provide correction, and or help one navigate their affairs in this life. They can often be critical to one's success.

Memory Verse *Revelation 2:29* He that hath an ear, let him hear what the spirit saith unto the churches

Biblical Application

In *John 6:63* Jesus said, "the words that I speak unto you, they are spirit, and they are life" Which allows man to understand that God's written word is spirit and is sufficient to give one all that is needed for this life. So, when God reveals something through one's spiritual senses, it should serve as a compliment to the written word. God's revelation will never be contradictory to the written word. This lesson in not designed to have individuals running and looking to hear voices or looking to see deeper through natural things in every circumstance, but it is a reminder that God can and does reveal beyond the natural. What a believer can do if God chooses to reveal something, is to place themselves in a posture that God can entrust that person with the revealed information. The posture for the believer is one of devotion, which includes prayer, study and meditation on His word.

God's Spiritual Revelations

- Anna & Simeon. *Luke 2:25-28.*
- Elijah. *I Kings 17: 2:16, 18:41.*
- Elisha. *II Kings 6: 12-17.*
- Peter. *Acts 10: 10-16.*
- Phillip. *Acts 8: 26-35.*

Everyday Life Application

Testify to a time when the Spirit of God spake or allowed you to see, that helped you (whether a warning or job offer or a present evil etc.) on you journey or in your understanding.

Author: Elder James Taylor, Jr.

Lesson 43 July 29, 2023
Av 11, 5783

OPPRESS THE HIRELING IN HIS WAGES

Introduction

Wages for most private sector workers in the U.S. rose at least 5% from the second quarter of 2020 through second quarter of 2021 (Pew Research).[10] However, the official U.S. poverty rate in 2020 was 11.4%, up 1% from 10.5 % in 2019(Census). As of 2020, 1.5% of hourly paid workers still earn the federal minimum wage of $7.25 hour or less (BLS). Many corporations view minimizing pay and benefits to workers as a means to increase profits as sound business. Covetousness and greed is often rationalized in corporate America. From 1978 to 2020, CEO pay grew by 1,322% while wages of an average worker grew 18% (EPI). The Bible addresses the unrighteous oppression of workers.

Memory Verse *Malachi 3*:5 And I will come near to you to judgment; and I will be a swift witness against the sorcerers, and against the adulterers, and against false swearers, and against those that oppress the hireling in his wages, the widow, and the fatherless, and that turn aside the stranger from his right, and fear not me, saith the LORD of hosts.

Biblical Application

---

[10] https://www.pewresearch.org/fact-tank/2021/12/22/many-u-s-workers-are-seeing-bigger-paychecks-in-pandemic-era-but-gains-arent-spread-evenly/
https://www.bls.gov/opub/reports/minimum-wage/2020/home.htm
https://www.census.gov/library/publications/2021/demo/p60-273.html
https://www.epi.org/

According to *I Timothy 5:18,* the laborer is worthy of his reward. God cares about the wages of workers. Those who oppress(defraud) the hireling, widow, and the fatherless will receive the same judgment as those who commit adultery or sorcery. Rich men who fraudulently keep back the hire (pay) of workers are told to weep and howl for the miseries that shall come upon them. The cries of those workers entered into the ear of the Lord of Sabaoth (armies). *Jeremiah 22:-3* Woe unto him that buildeth his house by unrighteousness, and his chambers by wrong; that useth his neighbor's service without wages, and giveth him not for his work. If we utilize our neighbor's service, we should be careful to pay them equitably for their work. As followers of Christ, we can give glory to God through the treatment of those who work for us. Let us ensure that we engage in righteous practices in our work and towards those we are fortunate enough to employ.

- Oppress not the hireling. *Malachi 3:1-6; Deuteronomy 24:14-15 Leviticus 19:13.*
- Build in righteousness. *Jeremiah 22:13-17; James 5:1-6; Proverbs 22:16; 14:31.*

Everyday Life Application

Testify about how the Lord has blessed you in your work and business. Have you had to take a stand against unrighteous wage practices in your workplace?

Lesson 44 August 5, 2023
Av 18, 5783

THE POWER OF FRIENDSHIP

Introduction

Thank you for being a friend. Travel down the road and back again. Your heart is true, you are a pal and a confidant. And if you threw a party, invited everyone you knew. You would see the biggest gift would be from me and the card attached would say, thank you for being a friend. Sound familiar? The theme song from the hit TV show, The Golden Girls, captures the blessing of having a friend. One of the greatest examples of friendship in the scripture is the friendship that existed between David and Jonathan *(I Samuel 18:1-5).* A real friend will be there for you no matter the situation. The wonderful thing for the believer is no matter the day or hour, we have a friend in Jesus. We serve a God who never slumbers nor sleeps (*Psalms 121*:1). We have a God who is there to listen, encourage and take us through our most difficult and trying times. Be assured there is no friend like Jesus. What a friend we have in Jesus, all our sins and griefs to bear, what a privilege to carry everything to God in prayer. As you go through this lesson, consider what type of friend you are and ask yourself, what can you do to show yourself friendly.

Memory Verse *Proverbs 18:24* A man who has friends must himself be friendly, but there is a friend who sticks closer than a brother.

Biblical Application

There are many attributes of a real friend, and we could develop an exhaustive list of them. However, many would agree a real friend is one who is a good listener, is empathetic, loyal, dependable, and loves us for being our authentic self. There are many more you can name but in essence, a true friend is there when you need them, and they tell you the truth no matter what.

• A true friend tells you the truth and desires to make you better. *Proverbs 27:5-6, 27:17 9:8-10.*

• Real friends go the extra mile. *Mark 2:1-8.* (Explore this text)

1. How do you think the man with palsy felt about his friend's effort to get him to Jesus?

2. They carried him, took off the roof and lowered him down. What does this reveal about these men?

• From servant to friend. Jesus shares life wisdom. *John 15:11-17*

Everyday Life Application

In his book, "Leave Ordinary Behind" author Lance Witt ask a compelling question: Do you have a 2:00 a.m. friend? If you were in a crisis or desperate – who would you call? Call this friend today and thank them for being a friend.

Author: Deacon Walter H. Preston, Jr.

Lesson 45 August 12, 2023
Av 25, 5783

SURVIVING A PATMOS EXPERIENCE

Introduction

Patmos, a once flourishing island declined when it was conquered by the Romans. The Island was used as a place of exile for convicts. This is how Apostle John came to be there, *exiled by the Roman Emperor Titus Flavius Domitianus in 95 AC.* Apostle John was banished to this island for the word of God, and for the testimony of Jesus Christ (Revelation 1:9). He was not able to witness freely the message of Jesus Christ in his customary fashion, however, that did not stop the message. There is no record of John mummering or complaining about finding himself in this situation. However, he records in one instance he was in the spirit on the Lord's Day (Revelation 1:10)! Apostle John's response to his situation teaches that in whatever circumstances we may find ourselves, we can still remain productive in Jesus Christ.

Memory Verse *Matthew 7: 24* Therefore whosoever heareth these sayings of mine, and doeth them, I will liken him unto a wise man, which built his house upon a rock:

Biblical Application

The disciples spent much time being taught the message of salvation through Jesus Christ. Not only that, but to expect persecution in this world (Matthew 5:12-16). The disciples were alerted that the world would hate them as it had hated him (John 15:18), As a result, Apostle John's was not broken because of his Patmos experience,[11] but continued his assignment to spread the gospel (Rev. 1:13). This had to be a testament to Jesus Christ being

[11] https://www.greeka.com/dodecanese/patmos/history/

the foundation he stood on. The pandemic was such an experience for many of us. We were moved from our normal place of worship and comfort. However, God in his word shows us how not to be broken in our Patmos experience.

- We've been informed. *Romans 15:4; John 16: 33; I Peter 4: 12-19; II Timothy 3:12-17; I Thessalonians 5: 16-18.*
- The foundation matters. *Matthew 7: 21-27.*
- House built on the sand. *Mark 4: 3-7, 14-19.*
- House built on the rock. *Mark 4: 8-9, 20.*
- Having the right perspective. *Philippians 4: 10-13.*

Everyday Life Application

This Pandemic has been an eye opener to where we stand with God. What areas did you find were your strength and what areas need attention? What will you do moving forward, to ensure you are ready for a similar event if need be?

Author: *Evangelist Patricia Powell*

Lesson 46 August 19, 2023
Elul 2, 5783

TRUE WORSHIP

Introduction

Strong's Exhaustive Concordance of The Bible, defines "worship" as an act of reverence. The most common Greek word for worship is *proskyneo, which* is defined as, "to kiss the hand to (towards) one, in token of reverence. "True Worship", as described in Scripture, is focused entirely on the Lord (Deut. *26:10; 2 Ki. 17:36). The Lord is Holy (1 Chron. 16:29; Psa. 29:2*). The power of God's voice is seen and heard in scripture. The voice of the Lord is upon the waters: the God of glory thundereth: the Lord is upon many waters. The voice of the Lord is powerful; the voice of the Lord is full of majesty. God is worthy of worship (kneeling) because He is the Creator of all people (*Psa. 95: 6; 100:3*). God is Holy; He is to be feared. He deserves Godly reverence (*Psa. 96:9; 99:5; Zec. 14:17)*

Memory Verse: *Matthew 4:10* Then saith Jesus unto him, Get thee hence, Satan: for it is written, Thou shalt worship the Lord thy God, and him only shalt thou serve.

Biblical Application

"Worship" is the theme of Scripture from Genesis to Revelation. It is significant that Jesus spoke of *truth* as the distinctive mark of true worship. His word is truth. True worship always focuses on *who God is*. God is a Spirit and they that worship him must worship *him* in spirit and in truth. True worshipers will worship the Father in spirit and truth (*John 4: 20 – 26; John 17: 16-17*). Scripture contains directives and guidance for biblical worship. Scripture should guide our worship.

- Reverence for God. *Exodus 3:5; Joshua 5:15; Psalm 4:4, 33:8, 89:7, Habakkuk. 2:20.*
- Worship of Christ. *Matthew 2:11, 14:33, 28:9; Luke 24:52; Hebrews 1:6; Revelation 5:8.*
- Reverence for Christ. *Matthew 8:2, 9:18, 15:25, 20:20; Mark 5:22, 7:25*~~*; Joshua 9:38.*~~
- Spiritual worship required. *John 4: 21 – 24.*
- The Angel has the everlasting Gospel. *Revelation 14: 6-7.*
- Worship God *Revelation 15: 4, 19: 4, 10; 22: 8, 9.*

Everyday Life Application

Study God's word. Show reverence for God and sacred things. Cultivate true worship practices. Worship as God commands.

Author: Evangelist Irene Crawford

Lesson 47 August 26, 2023
Elul 9, 5783

WHEN I CONSIDER

Introduction

Have you taken the time to gaze into the sky on a clear night away from the lights of the city? Perhaps you have had the opportunity to examine the heavens using a telescope. When you look at the heavens what does it cause you to think about? Earth is one of the planets in a galaxy known as the Milky Way. A galaxy is defined as a huge collection of gas, dust, and billions of stars along with their solar systems that are held together by gravity. The Milky Way is just one of the estimated 100 billion galaxies in the universe. There are over 200 billion stars in our galaxy. Our solar system is composed of 8 primary planets and one star known as the sun. The sun is 93 million miles from Earth. (NASA)[12]. The vastness of the heavens speaks to the amazing power and glory of our Creator, the Lord God Almighty.

Memory Verse *Psalm 8:3* When I consider thy heavens, the work of thy fingers, the moon and the stars, which thou hast ordained;

Biblical Application

David looked at the heavens and glory of God's creation and declared his awe and utter amazement of God! The expression, "In all the earth," likely referred to his experiences as a shepherd and as soldier. As both, David had spent many nights considering the moon and stars leading him to conclude the excellence (majesty, greatness) of the Lord's name. The heavens (sky), the moon, and stars were set in place by the fingers of God (Strong's Dictionary). The Lord gave man dominion over the earth. The beasts of the field,

[12] https://spaceplace.nasa.gov/

birds of the air, and the creatures of the sea have been made subject to man. We see this dominion in the use of beasts, birds, and sea creatures for food, entertainment, and research. The fact that God put all things under the feet of man is also seen in science and medicine. David did not see many of the marvels of modern technology. However, he likely experienced God through his creation in a more intimate and vivid way than many of us. His experience generated a question about why a majestic and omnipotent God is mindful of and visited man. Instead of following the trend of modern humanism in self-worship and egoism; may God grant us grace and humility to reach the same conclusion of the psalmist. O Lord, our Lord, how excellent is thy name in all the earth.

- Consider the glory of God. *Psalm 8: 1-9, 19:1-6.*
- The Lord alone spreadeth out the heavens. *Job 9:1-15.*
- From everlasting to everlasting, thou art God. *Psalm 90:1-10.*

Everyday Life Application

In what other ways does the creation of God give glory to his name? What does the Bible call those who say there is no God?

Lesson 48 September 2, 2023
Elul 16, 5783

FORFEITING A GODLY HERITAGE

Introduction

Often in the scripture, there is a common theme of God introducing himself to an individual and from that point, being introduced to the offspring of that individual. An example would be God introducing himself to Abraham, and is now the God of Abraham, Isaac and Jacob (*Genesis 50:24*). This has been the case from ancient times until these modern times. Many believers today have obtained a heritage of Godliness that has been passed down from their forefathers. By definition, a heritage is an inheritance that is received from one's parent or ancestors, which can be spiritual or material (The Student Bible Dictionary.) A Godly heritage is so important because it influences one's identity, contributes to Godly characteristics, and distinguishes one from other groups, deities and customs. With God being the one that meets all needs (provider, sustainer, deliverer, protector, etc.) to have Him as one's heritage is something that is to be cherished and is invaluable.

Memory Verse *Luke 15:13* And not many days after the younger son gathered all together and took his journey into a far country and there wasted his substance with riotous living.

Biblical Application

Though invaluable, it is not uncommon for a Godly heritage to be squandered, devalued, or even forfeited. Because of the allure of the world (lust of the eyes, lust of the flesh and pride of life) and the attraction of other customs, beliefs, and ideologies, mankind has been guilty of being led astray from the will and purpose of God. This is the reason why God told Israel to not intermingle with the other nations upon entering the promised land. A decision that had nothing to do with race but was based on worship. Intermingling with these nations, was the very thing that led to idol worship and continues to be an issue in the body of Christ today. For many believers have, and are forfeiting their Godly heritage, which can and will eventually lead to their destruction.

In the Natural

- The value of heritage. *Proverbs 13:22; Psalms 127:3.*

Forfeiting the Inheritance

- Prodigal son. *Luke 15:11-24; Judges 2:7-10; I Samuel 8:1-9; I Kings 11:1-11; Romans 1:19-32.*

Valuing a Godly Heritage

- *Joshua 24:1-15.*

Everyday Life Application

In what way do you see Godly heritage being forfeited?

Author: Elder James Taylor, Jr.

Lesson 49 September 9, 2023
Elul 23, 5783

THE WISDOM OF GOD

Introduction

I have heard it said that smart people learn from their mistakes, but wise people learn from the mistakes of others. Wisdom is such a powerful and precious gift God gives to those who desire it. Wisdom is the application of knowledge to real life situations and circumstances. With all the access to information we have today, it is essential we never lose the desire to gain the wisdom of God. The wisdom of God is that God brings about the best possible results for the most possible people in the best possible way. God has always desired the best for his people, and this is evident in that he gave his best in his son Jesus. In his book The Knowledge of the Holy, A.W. Tozer states, "Wisdom, among other things, is the ability to devise perfect ends and to achieve those ends by the most perfect means. It sees the end from the beginning, so there can be no need to guess or conjecture... All God's acts are done in perfect wisdom, first for His own glory, and then for the highest and greatest good for the greatest number for the longest time...Not only could His acts not be done better: a better way to them could not be imagined. No wonder the writer of Jude says, To the only wise God our Saviour, be glory and majesty, dominion, and power, both now and ever. Amen. *(Jude 1:25)*

Memory Verse *Romans 11:33-34* O the depth of the riches both of the wisdom and knowledge of God! how unsearchable are his judgments, and his ways past finding out! For who~~m~~ hath known the mind of the Lord? or who hath been his counsellor?

Biblical Application

In many of the Proverbs there is a comparison between being wise and being foolish. The writer encourages us to pursue and desire to have wisdom. In *Proverbs 9:10,* it says The fear of the LORD is the beginning of wisdom: and the knowledge of the holy is understanding. The Hebrew word for wisdom is hakma which means skill or applied knowledge. The book of Proverbs is meant to assist us in developing a set of practical skills for living well in God's world. It also helps us to live in a way that honors God and others. As we explore this lesson, let us seek to allow wisdom to speak to us and open our hearts to receive what she says to us.

- God is not holding back on giving us wisdom, ask for it. *James 1:5-6.*
- God desires for us to have wisdom. *Proverbs 2:1-7, Colossians 1:9-14.*
- Wise people receive instruction. *Proverbs 12:15, 19:20.*
- We must desire to live wisely. *Ephesians 5:15-17.*
- God's wisdom is beyond what we can comprehend. *I Corinthians 2:1-16.*
- Solomon's request was granted, and God gave him wisdom. *I Kings 3:7-28, 4:29-33.*

Everyday Life Application

Think about the greatest thing you are facing right now. How are you seeking God's wisdom to help you navigate and go through this situation? Discuss with the class.

Author: Deacon Walter H. Preston, Jr.

.

www.ingramcontent.com/pod-product-compliance
Lightning Source LLC
La Vergne TN
LVHW050314160826
845677LV00014B/3391

* 9 7 9 8 8 4 7 2 0 4 3 9 2 *